LOBBYIST OR BARBER

How The Right Relationships Can Build
A Strong Government Affairs Program

BOB KEATON

ISBN-13: 978-1983877216
ISBN-10: 1983877212

Special Acknowledgements

Little can be achieved in life without family and friends. Some of those people are not in this world, but they are still inspiring me every day. This book would not be possible without the constant love and support of my wife, Jennifer, from the very beginning.

Contents

INTRODUCTION
Debunking the Myths

L OBBYIST. GOVERNMENT AFFAIRS professional. Public affairs consultant.

The reputation of each of those words varies immensely, even though what they do surrounds the same goal: influencing public policy.

The term "lobbyist" evokes negative connotations, due to stories of scandals on K Street in Washington, D.C. and the inference that politicians can be bought off with lavish gifts, expensive travel—or even sizeable campaign contributions.

Whereas, the title of "government affairs professional" doesn't seem evil. Government affairs professionals are those whom you see attending legislative committee meetings, explaining government actions to corporate executives, and speaking on cable news programs.

The public affairs consultant is someone who sets up community meetings with local companies, invites elected officials to speak, and arranges a breakfast at your organization to become more acquainted with the issues.

This person seems even less sinister.

The fact is: All three of these professionals undertake a lot of the same roles and responsibilities. But the words used to describe them matter a great deal in how each one of them is portrayed, their credibility, and their overall effectiveness.

Did you know that some of the best-known national organizations whose mission involves a worthy cause—such as the American Heart Association—hire lobbyists?

But that wouldn't make you think any less of their purpose, would it?

The truth is—everybody and everything is impacted by the government—at each level. Whether the issue involves taxes, regulations, or public safety, every organization is effected by public policy. And whether that public policy favors you or not, you must have a seat at the table for your voice to be heard.

Using my nearly three decades of experience in campaigns, legislative policy, executive staffing, and lobbying, I created this book to serve as a guide into the world of government relations—an industry that takes each of the terms mentioned above and describes their roles and responsibilities—and how they can impact you and your organization.

PROLOGUE
Why Use "Lobbyist or Barber?"

WHEN I STARTED this book on government affairs, a challenge I encountered early on was how to convey my message in a title and make that message something everyone could relate to. After several drafts of the final manuscript, the title became apparent, and I immediately put it down on paper.

The next morning, I spoke with my wife, and her very first comment was, "Why would you use 'Lobbyist or Barber?'"

She went on to say that mentioning a barber does not make sense when talking about government affairs. That was a concern, and later that night—as I reflected—it came to me: the barbershop back home: the one owned by Rosie.

I grew up in a small town in Western Pennsylvania, and—like most steel towns—we suffered through a boom time and then a bust—much like the Great Depression. Family and friends lost their jobs, and we all wondered what would happen to us. These were very tough times, and—in many cases—these towns became ghost towns, never to recover to this day.

Growing up in a household with a sibling and my mother was

challenging, since we lost my father suddenly when I was six years old. Equally challenging was the fact that we had one car, which was used to get my mother back and forth to work and that was our only means of transportation. My transportation was either my feet or a bike.

So, I decided, at fifteen years of age, to get a job.

It is tough to find a job at that age, and harder still when you don't have wheels. Through contacts with friends and conversations, I stumbled upon a job working for a local barbershop in town: Bianco's Barber-Stylists.

Conveniently, the shop—owned by brothers Rosie and Ray Bianco—was about a mile from my home. My job was to clean the shop in the evenings and, on Saturdays, stop by to get them a pizza for lunch. The shop was a great gathering center to discuss politics, family, or the recent high school game. No matter the topic, Rosie or Ray would engage and seemed to know something about every subject of conversation.

Many times, I would go to the shop and see city council members, school administrators, or even the mayor waiting for a haircut and a chance to discuss the latest issues.

One day, I recall a very heated discussion on the recent high school football game with a crosstown rival. In the end, it was all in good humor—much like a debate you would have with family over a holiday bowl game.

I never realized the level of the networking that was taking place, or what that really meant, until a close friend of the family ran for a county row office.

That year, the candidate approached my mother about putting a campaign sign in our yard. She agreed, which was a big deal since she was not active politically. She was a Republican, and the candidate was a Democrat, but it did not matter to her since he was a friend. On election day, after the polls closed, we went to the house of the candidate for a party. The race was very close between our friend, the Democrat, and the Republican opponent.

I was too young to vote at the time, and not exactly sure of the process, but I saw people running in and out of the house with poll numbers to tabulate the returns. Everyone in town was standing in the kitchen, from the owner of the local car dealer down the road to the owner of a pizza shop, and—you guessed it—Rosie.

He was in the kitchen, tabulating numbers and leading the charge. My bet is he knew everyone in the room from the shop—and probably knew more than most about what was happening in their lives.

In the end, I learned a very valuable lesson: While you may not agree with a person in the room, you can still build a relationship with someone, simply by listening to their concerns. This is what a lobbyist does on a day-to-day basis and—like Rosie—they build relationships with those around them.

I've been lucky enough to have a long and fruitful career. I get to do what I love every day, and I've had the opportunity to do what I love for years. I get to help people, invest in causes that I believe in, and influence legislation and public policy. It's an incredible feeling to know that what I do each day has a direct and positive impact on the world around me.

I'm a lobbyist.

I started my venture in government by serving as the executive director of the Senate Veterans Affairs and Emergency Preparedness Committee, under former state Senator Terry Punt (R-Franklin County).

While on the committee, I worked on a variety of issues, including increased compensation for veterans and creating a flag for fallen volunteer firefighters. It was this experience that drew me into being able to help people, especially veterans and first responders, who I consider to be the real American heroes of our day.

From the State Senate, I was appointed by Governor Tom Ridge (who later became the nation's first secretary of Homeland Security) to act as a policy specialist for the Governor's Banking, Insurance, and Securities Policy Office.

While there, I developed Governor Ridge's policy agenda for each of those agencies. I provided input for a number of policy initiatives, including workers' compensation reform, managed-care reform, the Children's Health Insurance Program (Pennsylvania was the nation's first state to develop and implement CHIP before it became a national model), the Medical Malpractice Privatization Initiative, the Entrepreneurial Advisory Committee, the Pennsylvania Community Development Bank, and banking and insurance reform.

From there, I worked as a contract lobbyist, focusing on non-profit and health care clients. I crafted legislative strategies and coordinated capital activities for clients. These outreach efforts included both government relations and public affairs components, providing clients with the necessary vehicles for presenting their message to their constituencies, both inside and outside of the Capitol.

Eventually, I moved on to serve as the director of State Government Affairs for Sunoco: one of the largest independent refineries in the United States and the largest in the Northeast. In this capacity, I served as the primary contact for Sunoco in Pennsylvania, Oklahoma, and Texas. I represented Sunoco on association boards, hired lobbyists, and worked with the Departments of Environmental Protection and Transportation in each state. I handled community outreach regarding the refining, marketing, logistics, and petrochemical sectors of the company.

After working for Sunoco, I went on to work as the director of government affairs for two different nationally affiliated associations: one for architects and the other for small businesses.

As you can see, a professional lobbyist is required to be an expert in several different areas. A lobbyist must build relationships, research key issues, and be willing to know the facts—and use those facts to guide and influence policy.

Lobbyists represent all kinds of groups, including trade associations, special interest groups, and non-profits. Acting on behalf of non-profits and businesses alike, I have had the opportunity to help guide the hand of the legislative process. It's incredibly rewarding to know that I've played a part in making the world a better place.

Too often, whenever an organization, association, or corporation begins building a government relations or public affairs program, it gets so caught up in the branding that the human element is forgotten. I've written this book to help people understand and engage in the lobbying process at every level. Whether you are trying to figure out how lobbying can help further your interests in a general sense, or you have a specific issue that you are invested in, having a lobbyist on your side can assist you in building relationships, getting a seat at the table, and providing education and research to legislators.

The American democratic process invites participation from its constituents. A lobbyist knows the ins and outs of the systems of government and can guide you through this participation.

CHAPTER 1
What Is Lobbying?

"Lobbyists have more offices in Washington than the president. You see, the president only tells Congress what they should do. Lobbyists tell 'me what they will do."

Will Rogers,
American Humorist

THE TERM "LOBBYIST" dates back to the early 1800s, yet today it is still an extremely misunderstood profession.

As the American League of Lobbyists (ALL) celebrates its twentieth anniversary, we are all committed to increasing professionalism in the lobbying field. Our mission, as those who practice this craft, is to spend time this year educating the public about the value we as lobbyists bring to our legislative, political, and regulatory processes.

For too long, we have stayed silent about what we do.

A lobbyist with Miller/Wenhold Capitol Strategies and a former president of the American League of Lobbyists is challenging every lobbyist and organization listed in this book to defend their profession when it's attacked and to educate the public on the value we add to our system of government.

Why?

Every two years, lobbyists come under attack. We are blamed for all that is wrong in Washington, D.C. and throughout the country, as candidates seek out votes from unknowing constituents.

Why do candidates do this?

The answer is simple: attacking a profession not widely understood by the public not only sells newspapers, but it also gets votes. It's only after candidates win the election that they come calling, asking lobbyists to help financially through political action committee (PAC) contributions or to assist in lobbying for or against a pet project in their state or district. To some politicians, lobbyists are a necessary evil that allows them to get elected.[1]

To the general public, lobbyists are corrupt.

That isn't a promising picture of a profession that plays such a valuable role in our process; this is the perception of every lobbyist in Washington, D.C., and throughout every state capital. The challenge ALL face, from this year forward, is to provide better information about what a lobbyist is and does. What role a lobbyist play in:

- The legislative process?

- The political process?

- Their community?

There is some debate about the origination of the term "lobbyist." Some sources state that President Ulysses S. Grant first coined the term in the 1870s, in response to political activists who used to flock to him with agendas and questions in the lobby of the Willard Hotel in

---

1 Miller, Paul. "Lobbying: A Misunderstood Profession." An article, Washington Representatives Magazine 2005, Columbia Books, Inc. http://www.mwCapitol.com/news/lobbying/misunderstood.pdf

Washington, D.C. Others point to the year 1830 as the first time the word appeared in print, when used in connection with Ohio politics. [2]

Wherever the word came from, the meaning remains the same. A lobbyist is someone who builds networks and relationships with those who can influence the legislative process. Lobbying is often described as if it were a new phenomenon, when—in fact—it has been a reality of our democracy since at least the beginning of the twentieth century, and perhaps longer. Lobbying is considered an act of free speech, and it is protected by the First Amendment to the United States Constitution.

A lobbyist presents his or her case to lawmakers and argues in favor of the legislation that works in support of his or her organization.

Such was the case of the March of Dimes when lobbying was instrumental in passing laws to screen newborns for illnesses. Lawmakers don't always know every side of an issue, so it is up to a lobbyist to present his or her client's perspective.

TYPES OF LOBBYISTS

Several different types of lobbyists help certain groups: corporate, association, independent citizen, or grassroots lobbyists.

Ultimately, lobbyists cannot control how legislators will vote on an issue, but they can at least present them with another set of facts. Then legislators can consider the information when making their final decision.

CORPORATE LOBBYISTS

These lobbyists work for corporations, and they often educate government officials on how certain pieces of legislation may affect the business that employs them. A legislator may not realize the effects that new regulations or higher taxes may have on a company, or they may only have a vague idea of what the aftermath will be. Many elected

2 Headliner, Jesse. "A Lobbyist by Any Other Name?" Interview by Liane Hansen. Weekend Edition Sunday. NPR.org. 22 Jan. 2006. http://www-s4.npr.org/templates/story/story.php?storyId=5167187

officials have never worked in business, so corporate lobbyists can help educate them.

Corporate lobbyists can be in-house, meaning that the corporation employs them directly, so they can lobby on the behalf of the corporation. Or they can be consultant lobbyists, meaning that they are specifically hired from outside of the company to assist with specific issues and outreach. Many of these are employed, either full or part-time, by specific contract lobbying firms.

ASSOCIATION LOBBYISTS

Association lobbyists act in much the same way as corporate lobbyists: building relationships with lawmakers and representing the interests of a non-profit or similarly-structured organization.

For example, if the American Business Women's Association were to a hire a lobbyist, it might emphasize issues regarding equal pay, laws, or regulations regarding employer-sponsored health care for women.

The NAACP (National Association for the Advancement of Colored People) assists persons of color with progressing in their profession, community, or socioeconomic situations. They might hire a lobbyist if a law being considered might disproportionately affect people of color. The lawmakers developing the bill may not have realized the potential consequences, and a lobbyist can assist the association by presenting as to why the legislation should be voted down or modified.

These are just a couple of examples. Many other associations represent all sorts of groups: professional associations (such as the two previously mentioned), trade associations, environmental groups, and single-issue organizations like the NRA (National Rifle Association).

Associations are created to organize and unite like-minded people. A lobbyist can represent these groups—and attempt to influence legislation and public opinion on their behalf.

Independent Lobbyists

Also known as a "citizen lobbyist", an independent lobbyist does not work for a corporation and is not affiliated with any organization.

Many citizens choose to lobby because one or more issues deeply move them. The Affordable Care Act was one piece of legislation that many people felt very passionately about, both in favor of and in opposition to. Many citizen lobbyists have gotten involved with the process regarding this law and met with lawmakers, sent emails, and arranged meetings to state their case and their evidence, either for or against the ACA.

Just as a corporate or association lobbyist would do, citizen lobbyists may present research and statistics. They might rely on anecdotes or personal experiences, when appropriate. They may try to influence legislators to vote in a certain way, or they may suggest alternative solutions and ways that the legislation may be modified so constituents on both sides of the aisle are satisfied, and a consensus can be reached.

Grassroots Lobbyists

Grassroot lobbying takes place when an organization presents its case to the public and asks for involvement—from the grass up through the roots—so to speak.

Any time you see or hear an advertisement for a specific issue that ends by urging the audience to contact their legislator, it is an example of grassroots lobbying. MADD (Mothers Against Drunk Driving) is one non-profit organization that has successfully used a grassroots lobbying strategy to influence legislation.

Types of Outreach

A lobbyist may engage in three kinds of outreach: legislative, governmental, and public affairs.

LEGISLATIVE OUTREACH

Legislative outreach is important, because thousands of pieces of legislation are introduced each legislative cycle, but only a small percentage of these go on to become law.

Laws and regulations can help or hurt an organization. Legislative outreach involves monitoring legislation and keeping track of what bills are being proposed, modified, or coming up for vote. It also involves knowing where elected officials stand regarding a piece of legislation and knowing who is in favor of the bill, who is against it, and who is undecided.

The undecided representatives are the people on whom a lobbyist would focus their efforts. They may also meet with the representatives who will vote in a way that is favorable to your organization and ensure that their vote can be counted on.

A lobbyist may take some time to meet with those representatives who are in opposition to your organization's position and present your point of view. Even if it is a long shot, it's still worth taking the time, and it's all a part of building relationships with your elected officials.

GOVERNMENTAL OUTREACH

Governmental outreach is the relationship-building aspect of lobbying. To really advocate for an organization's interests, a lobbyist will get to know elected officials.

Having face-to-face meetings, sending emails, following up on previous communications, and attending events are all ways that a lobbyist may forge relationships on your behalf.

Nearly every business in America functions based on networking: the ability to increase your size through relationship-building. Developing strong networks takes time, money, and effort. A good lobbyist can maximize your resources and energy so that you can get results quickly.

Public Affairs

Public affairs is a bit different from the previous two forms of outreach, because it involves interacting with the public, rather than interacting with governmental officials. An excellent community outreach program is important, because it increases an organization's credibility and visibility in the community, and it can energize the public to create grassroots campaigns.

Not only that, but public policy can change the rhetoric of an issue and sway public opinion. If community perception is influenced enough, constituents may modify the way they vote and begin electing office representatives who are more in line with your organization's interests and values.

KEY TAKEAWAYS

- Lobbyist networks can build relationships to influence legislation and public opinion.

- There are four types of lobbyists: corporate, association, independent (citizen), and grassroots.

- There are three forms of outreach that a lobbyist may engage in: legislative, governmental, and public affairs.

- Legislative and governmental outreach are similar. Both deal with attempting to influence legislation at multiple levels. Legislative outreach is directly interacting with the legislation by keeping up with new bills, educating policy-makers on the effects of these bills, and suggesting modifications or changes. Governmental outreach is all about building relationships with elected officials.

- Public affairs uses a lobbyist's influence on, and relationship with, the public. A lobbyist may engage in public affairs in an attempt to educate the public on a specific issue or to sway community views.

CHAPTER 2
Lobbyists As Advocates

"Lobbyists' influence comes from access, not money."

President Barack Obama

A N EXPRESSION IN Washington, D.C., about advocating for a cause is: "You are either at the table or on the menu." In the world of politics, if you are not part of the conversation, your interests may be sacrificed. This might not even be purposefully done. It's like that old saying, "The squeaky wheel gets the oil."

If a bill is coming up for review that will negatively impact your business, and you do not have someone working on your behalf and acting as a part of the conversation, that bill may pass—without legislators even realizing it will have a disproportionately negative impact on businesses in your industry.

The upshot is: if you say nothing, then you have no opinion—and that can be very dangerous.

As fast as the world is changing and evolving, the world of lobbying (or advocating) is growing even more quickly. Being relevant means you are at the table and that you hold sway with the leaders who are driving change and making policy.

You hold sway or influence when you build a reputation as an expert in your field and when you make an effort to forge relationships with those in positions of power.

A familiar question asked by companies and associations is: "Why do we need a lobbyist?" Given the negative media attention in Washington, D.C., many people continue to ask this question.

Lobbying basically comes down to advocacy. A lobbyist will advocate for your organization's interests and values, form relationships, and keep abreast of new legislation and amendments to existing bills that might impact you. Developing contacts, networking among friends, getting people to pass your name along, and belonging to organizations of like-minded people are all fundamentals of networking and marketing. The same applies to lobbying.

Association, corporate, and contract lobbyists all strive to educate policy-makers on issues so that they can make informed decisions. With thousands of bills introduced each legislative session, staying on top of every item is very challenging. A lobbyist is a professional who can assist with this monumental task.

Advocacy happens every day across the country in town councils, county seats, state capitals, and in Washington, D.C.

Advocacy may be done on behalf of those who wish to raise the minimum wage, legalize the use of medical marijuana, or simply install a new stop sign on a busy residential street.

All issues require some form of advocacy. Simply put, these issues need lobbying. Doctors, lawyers, car dealers, business owners, and all other professionals flock to state capitals each year to advocate for their interests. They all want to make their voices heard and contribute to the conversation surrounding legislation.

Associations may send advocates to their state capital to speak about the issues that are important to them. While being able to express a position and verbally elocute with confidence is incredibly important regarding advocacy, it is equally vital that you establish your goals and state what it is you want to achieve.

If you are opposed to an issue or bill, just saying no for the sake of saying no accomplishes nothing. You must also be willing to put forth alternative ideas or a compromise. Finding a way around a challenge or concern improves your case. (This is far more efficient when done in conjunction with determining your organization's strategy.)

From there, you would decide how you want to communicate with legislators. You would consider options such as holding a press event or rally, scheduling face-to-face meetings, launching a letter-writing campaign, or finding someone to speak on your organization's behalf.

Finally, make sure you plan your activities several months in advance, with an outline covering the place, date, and time. You need to give yourself ample time to organize and create buzz around your events. You may want to send a word out to your organization's members or partner with associations that have goals similar to yours.

To further your influence, you may even find yourself partnering with organizations outside your industry, seeing they are willing to support your cause or act as an ally.

You also want to give yourself time to plan for things to go wrong and deal with any potential roadblocks, such as the cancellation of session days, a major breaking news story that will divert time and attention, or competing legislation that takes center stage. Have contingencies set in place and make sure that you have enough time to enact them, should any part of your plan fall apart. This could be something as simple as inclement weather the day of your press event, another hot-button issue that takes attention away from your organization's position, or a key position lawmaker—who was previously your ally—changing his or her position.

It's important to keep in mind that even if you have provided a strong effort and are conscientious in your development, sometimes advocacy just doesn't go as planned. You must take these lessons and learn from them.

Case in point:

Several years ago, I worked on behalf of a manufacturing training facility. The school was created to provide students with specific skills and help them prepare for a career in a trade industry. On paper, the school looked great and had a very high job-placement rating, providing top notch training for students. Parents loved the school and admissions grew each year.

Unfortunately, all of the success was superficial. Underneath lie a vast array of serious financial issues, with no solution in sight.

When I first started working with this client, I contacted the Pennsylvania Department of Labor and Industry to get an idea as to where we could locate funding to help ease the school's financial burden.

Timing was not on our side. We were at the end of a gubernatorial administration, with a new governor of the opposite political party taking the oath of office in a few weeks. Those within the governor's administration, who had pushed for the organization from the beginning, would be leaving with the change of power.

Our advocates would soon be out of jobs themselves.

Further complicating matters, administrative decisions at the school had jeopardized federal dollars: the funds had not been properly allocated.

But we continued our campaign.

Parents, teachers, and faculty contacted legislators to garner support. The Pennsylvania House Majority Policy Committee held a hearing at the school, and the local press covered the event. State senators from the region also vocalized their support. The school had connections with the mayor and other leaders in the community. As far as advocacy goes, we garnered the support of most of the key players.

We had all the pieces in place to make our case, except for the most important part: MONEY.

The biggest issue the school faced was the state budget. That year, Pennsylvania's government faced a very difficult budget, and the money was just not there for the new governor to support the school. In fact, the budgeting process didn't go as planned. Some of the budget passed early, and the education funding portion wasn't resolved until Christmas—six months too late.

As you can see, lobbying is not a guarantee that your organization's needs will be met. Because of circumstances beyond my client's control, our strategy wasn't a sure success. But it did stack the odds a bit more in our favor, because—when the next budget cycle came around—policy-makers and legislators already knew about our issue and challenges and were more apt to help.

When you are trying to accomplish something, you want to take advantage of every resource that you have at your disposal.

Lobbying is a resource.

There is no reason why you should not take hold of this valuable tool.

Sometimes, however, money isn't the largest obstacle.

Often efforts to enhance public safety—which many would think would elicit a great deal of support—aren't as easy as you would think. During a corporate government affairs meeting at Sunoco, I was told of an issue with shutoff valves for our gas stations. Convenience stores like Sheetz, WAWA, Rutter's, 7-Eleven, and Circle K were being impacted by what could be a serious safety threat. Multiple convenience stores— some with as many as ten fuel pumps—had only one shutoff valve if there was an accident or fire at the pump.

Just imagine if a small fire were to start at a gas station. It would take valuable seconds for a store employee to notice and come outside to hit the shutoff valve—or a quick-responding customer to eventually locate the button to turn off the flow of gas. Clearly, this was a huge public safety issue and a priority for my company, and we wanted more than one shutoff valve in the case of an emergency.

- Why couldn't the company just install new shutoff valves?

- Was state action required?

It was my job to find out.

My first call was to the Pennsylvania Department of Labor and Industry to see what we would need to do to make the change.

Was this a regulatory or a legislative issue?

I met with the secretary of Labor and Industry and other department leaders to discuss the issue at hand. During the meeting, they advised me that the solution had to be legislative—meaning a change in state law—and it would need support from the industry.

Drafting legislation and getting industry support was a tall order. With a two-year legislative cycle and about half the session gone, we had a short timeframe. Once I left the meeting, I needed to find a legislative champion who understood fire safety—and I knew just the guy.

I called the go-to legislator—a volunteer firefighter—to ask him to co-sponsor our legislation. (It later turned out that after he left the Legislature, he became the state's fire commissioner. So, I apparently picked the right guy.)

When I called him, he immediately agreed, and a bill went for drafting that same day. The next steps were to reach out to the convenience store association to get approval, to work on co-sponsors for the legislation, and to meet with the chairmen of the legislative committees to highlight the importance of this—if it was going to have any chance of passing.

The bill was introduced with co-sponsors about three weeks later, and my next meeting was with the committee chairs. During our meeting with the committee, legislators agreed this was a safety issue, but universal agreement suggested we needed the backing of the industry before the committee would move the legislation.

(I must add that right after this meeting, my wife and I went on vacation to San Diego. While we were in the middle of a wine tasting in the Temecula Valley, my phone rang. Yes, I answered the phone— so, I am a good lobbyist, but maybe not so good in the Husband Department).

During the call, I was told by our contract lobbyist that it looked like the bill was on hold, because the budget was not going to pass on time and that was the focus of House and Senate activity that fall. When we returned from vacation—and a long flight back—I reached out to stores and the Convenience Store Association.

Naturally, I thought everyone would be in support, but nothing could be further from the truth. There were many questions:

- How far away would the additional shutoff valve be from the main shutoff?

- What would the cost be to a store?

- And why?

These questions had to be answered in less than three months or the legislation was never going to move.

You guessed it—the legislation did not pass that session. In fact, it did not pass for another two years, when I was in another position in a different organization.

Just like any tool, lobbying is ineffective if not correctly put into practice. You want to utilize it in the most efficient manner possible and not leave anything to chance—so get out ahead of the issues.

Do everything you can to ensure your message is heard.

One way you can guarantee you are fully taking advantage of lobbying and enacting it to its greatest potential is to form a political action committee (PAC).

A well-managed PAC allows for companies, or individuals within an association, to pool their resources and maximize their giving potential. PACs, like anything else, can be mismanaged and misused; however, they can be a useful tool.

And I have learned that not having one can make your organization invisible.

While en route to Austin, Texas for a routine business trip at Sunoco very early in the morning, I received a text from our corporate communications director. Our company had a problem. A front-page news story in Houston showed a sinkhole with approximately thirty pipelines, several of which had burst. We had a pipeline that was in that hole, and Corporate wanted to get out ahead of the story.

It may not be a shock to some, but most government employees don't start their days before 9 a.m., so I had some planning to do before the day started.

My very first call was to the governor's office in Texas, informing his emergency response team we were on the issue and would get back to them ASAP. Next, I called and left a message with the Texas Railroad Commission, the agency with oversight of pipelines.

Fortunately, I had met two of the railroad commissioners at an Energy Council meeting a few months earlier, and they were familiar with my name. Once both were contacted, I called local officials, including those at the state and federal levels, so they knew we were on top of the situation. Finally, I called Corporate Communications back, so they knew what was happening and could contact local news outlets.

Giving the elected officials a bit of lead time allowed them to react thoughtfully and strategically when called by citizens or the media.

Before I was hired, we had very little presence in Texas and little or no outreach from our PAC. Compared to other very large energy PACs, we were the unwanted stepsister. With my help, we were able to develop relationships with the main people who gave us access to the helpful individuals in this situation.

What eventually happened?

After everyone was contacted, I called our pipeline offices to see about identifying the pipeline.

Was this going to be a big clean up?

I was told our company was in the process of using technology to identify the specific pipeline in the sinkhole. Within two hours, I was called back—this time by our communications office—and told our pipeline was all right and there were no issues. That was a big relief for everyone involved—especially the community members.

In any event, we were on top of the situation and demonstrated to elected officials in the community that we were also willing to share with them not-so-great information and were not hiding anything from them.

In public affairs, staying on top of these issues will make or break your reputation: people want to know what is happening without all the smoke and mirrors.

I reached back to the governor's office, the Railroad Commission, and the elected officials to give them the update before they saw it on the news. This is not always easy to do, but how you handle a communication issue with those in government is equally important. I was successful in reaching out to these people because I had previously engaged them in a PAC.

The main value of a PAC is that it allows an organization to establish relationships with elected officials, who ultimately decide the policy that will directly impact the bottom line. PACs can contribute to supporting candidates who are likely to vote in favor of certain pieces of legislation.

We'll talk more about PACs in a later chapter. For now, keep in mind that a PAC is necessary if you want to get the most from your advocacy efforts. Whether you are a corporation, a non-profit, or any other type of organization, a lobbyist can help get your agenda in front of policy-makers and present it in a way that makes sense—and translates directly into public policy.

Some of the ways that lobbyists can assist corporations are by advocating against excessive regulations or bills that will hurt a company's profits. For example, in the year 2013, lobbyists representing the firm Citigroup played a key role in drafting additions to the bill H.R.992, which would have amended the Dodd-Frank Wall Street Reform and Consumer Protection Act.

These lobbyists reviewed the proposal, suggested amendments, and even wrote a couple of paragraphs that ended up being added to the bill. The lobbyists worked to limit regulations that would hurt profits in the financial industry. [3]

Medicare Part D is another piece of legislation that was influenced heavily by lobbyist activity. The bill was introduced in the year 2000.

------

3 Yglesias, Matthew. "Why Lobbyists Write Bills and Why You Shouldn't Worry Too Much About It." Slate.com. 24, May 2013.

It bans bulk purchasing, which saves medical companies billions of dollars a year. [4]

Lobbyists can also be instrumental in furthering the interests of non-profit and trade organizations.

Lobbyists advocate for non-profits by paying attention to legislation regarding taxes and anything that may impact the rules and qualifications of a non-profit's tax-exemption status. They also advocate on behalf of bills that may have an impact on employment, or funding and grants made available to non-profit agencies. [5]

When it comes to enlisting the help of a lobbyist, it's important to be proactive. If you wait until there is a problem and you only react, you may not get the results that you want. Instead of waiting until you are in desperate need, hire an in-house contract lobbyist in advance.

If your organization employs an in-house lobbyist, they would research issues that relate to your organization, build connections, and form relationships on your behalf.

Then, when a problem does arise, or there is a piece of legislation or an issue where it is necessary to have the voice of your organization heard, a lobbyist can be ready to help. Your lobbyist will already have put the name of your organization in front of policy-makers and done all that they could to bolster your reputation and reach.

On the other hand, if you wait, you could end up having trouble getting your organization's voice heard. Yes, if your house catches on fire, you call the fire department. But it's always better to invest in fire prevention methods and keep it from happening in the first place. Think about it: houses burn down all the time. Sometimes by the time the fire department arrives, the flames are just too big.

By then, there isn't any way to reverse the damage.

Lobbying is a lot like that. Having a lobbyist acting as your advocate

4   Drutman, Lee. "How Corporate Lobbyists Conquered
American Democracy." The Atlantic.com. 20, April 2015
https://www.theatlantic.com/business/archive/2015/04/
how-corporate-lobbyists-conquered-americanan-democracy/390822/
5   "Public Policy Agenda." National Council of Non-profits. coun☒ilofnonprofits.
org. March 2017, p. 22.

all along is your way of preventing any figurative fires that need to be put out.

For instance, in the early 1990s, a prominent business in Harrisburg needed help.

It was dangerously close to having to shut down operations. The business sought out help, but—by that point—changing the tide of the outcome was next to impossible. Building strong relationships over a period of time might have contributed to saving the company. But because they waited until there was a major problem, they were not able to change the outcome.

Ultimately, all of their efforts failed.

The bottom line is that even if you have the best intentions, you just don't have the time to keep up with all the many pieces of legislation while also networking and building relationships on your organization's behalf. Only a professional lobbyist has the time and experience necessary to effectively advocate for your organization's platform.

Many times, a lobbyist will bring an impressive skill set with them, in addition to established relationships and contacts with lawmakers already formed over the course of their career. A lobbyist's good standing in the community and the political arena is necessary, because legislators are likely to listen and take advice from people whom they already know and trust.

Also, lobbyists can be active when the issue seems like a slam-dunk but becomes complicated quickly, such as in my next example.

In the course of their business, architects sign and seal documents in Pennsylvania for commercial buildings and multi-level structures, like townhomes. This is done to ensure safety, and—like an engineer— architects understand the fundamentals of both form and function.

When I lobbied for an association of architects, we faced an issue in which interior designers felt they should be licensed, like architects, to sign and seal drawings. The designers felt that they understood architectural principles, and many worked with architects on a day-to-day basis. They also felt that, many times, their training was better than some of the architects they worked with on projects.

Although the interior designers may have had a rational argument, the real issue was whether they had the prerequisite training and ability to operate as an architect.

Would that contradict studying to be an architect?

Paralegals can make this same argument. They have not been admitted to the bar to sign a docket, and—therefore—they cannot act as attorneys.

Or apply this analogy to health care. A nurse practitioner isn't the same as a doctor.

From a policy viewpoint, we felt we had won the issue—it was clearly about safety, not protecting the profession. An interior designer may do a terrific job picking out the right furniture, wall colors, and lighting, but do they have the education and training to know if a wall (that's blocking their design) can be safely removed?

From a lobbying perspective, the issue gets fuzzy. The state-wide interior designer association hired a high-profile lobbyist, who kept making the ability to sign and seal an issue and pushed for an informational hearing with the appropriate legislative committee.

The problem with such a discussion is that it opens a matter up to many other issues that may not even be related to the topic, and—many times—it rehashes an old argument for which a solution may have already been developed.

During the hearing, all sides were heard, and many legislators were—again—engaged on this issue and asking questions. But this time, lawmakers wanted a compromise.

Sometimes in the legislative process, a compromise is used to ask for the impossible—or kill a bill.

In this case, some of the committee members wanted a compromise, but luckily, the committee chairman was on our side.

Over the course of the prior couple of years, we had focused our efforts on the chair of the committee. We attended meetings and provided her with information. We even made her a PAC priority, ensuring that we had access to her. This was very important, because the lobbying firm hired by the interior designers did the same thing, and that was very likely the reason for the hearing in the first place.

One day, near the end of a legislative session—when all unpassed legislation is put on the governor's desk to die—I was asked by the executive director of the same committee about scheduling a meeting with the interior designers. I indicated we would need to get a go-ahead from both our national association and our state board of directors to authorize any meeting.

In the end, we never met, and the issue faded away.

If we had not had these relationships, interior designers would have been able to be considered the same as architects.

When looking for the answer to the question, "Why do we need a lobbyist?", it is critical to remember that a lobbyist can help a business become stronger.

Lobbyists work hard to build quality relationships with lawmakers.

THE ROLE OF A LOBBYIST AS A SOCIAL ADVOCATE

Lobbyists are key figures in the political process who use a combination of political contacts, persuasion, and public relations skills to represent the interests of organizations such as corporations, charities, and labor unions. They influence legislation.

Although sometimes portrayed as operators who push for laws that benefit narrow interests at the expense of the general public, lobbyists can—and sometimes do—serve as advocates for social issues related to education, health, and safety as well.

IDENTIFICATION

A Marquette University study of lobbying defines the activity as "advocating public relations", with "advocacy" defined as representing an individual, organization, or idea and persuading others to accept the viewpoints of the entity being represented.

Lobbyists represent the views of corporate and non-profit clients by providing information to lawmakers, influencing public opinion on issues that affect their clients, and creating alliances to support or oppose specific proposed laws. Organizations advocating social issues employ lobbyists, many of whom are former legislators or have extensive political contacts, to advocate for these issues.

POTENTIAL

Although non-profits have long used lobbyists to advocate for social issues, the Stanford Social Innovation Review at Stanford University reports that corporate lobbyists, because of the powerful influence they often exert in the legislative process, have greater potential than non-profits to influence legislators' votes on an array of social issues.

The publication cited cosmetics giant Mary Kay and its work to reduce violence against women as an example.

In 2005, six of the company's top sales directors drove to Washington, D.C., to urge Congress to reauthorize the Violence Against Women Act. By teaming up with other lobbyists and advocates, Mary Kay's efforts were successful.

In another example, Stanford reported that the Cartoon Network launched a campaign to increase recess periods in schools, allowing more exercise time for children to help reduce childhood obesity.

FEATURES

Lobbyists advocate for social causes by breaking down complex policy issues for lawmakers and legislative staff members, who often lack time to research these matters fully. They also can coordinate their efforts with those of other lobbyists and organizations advocating similar positions, thus increasing their clout with legislators. Lobbying tactics include organizing telephone, email, or letter-writing campaigns that encourage members of organizations they represent, and the general public, to contact elected representatives, asking them to vote a particular way.

CONSIDERATIONS

According to the Stanford Social Innovation Review, successful lobbying efforts by corporations have convinced many non-profits that they can best influence legislation on social issues by employing registered lobbyists with political clout and strong advocacy skills. Although lobbyists can be powerful forces in advocating for social causes, their influence does not come cheaply.

Stanford also reported that US corporations spent more $2.5 billion on lobbying expenses in 2006 alone, far more than the $222 million spent by non-profits between 1998 and 2004.

KEY TAKEAWAYS

A lobbyist will help an organization in three primary ways:

1. A lobbyist will keep abreast of legislation that is being written, coming up for a vote, or being amended.

2. A lobbyist will build a network and form relationships on your organization's behalf.

3. A lobbyist will present your organization's views and advocate on your behalf.

- Lobbying is advocacy: a lobbyist will promote the needs of your organization.

- Far too many pieces of legislation are introduced each year to keep up with—without the help of an experienced lobbyist.

- Lobbying is not a guarantee of success. It is the legislators themselves who make the final calls.

- Forming a PAC (political action committee) is something that should be done in conjunction with lobbying. It is a way for like-minded people or organizations to pool their money.

- A lobbyist can help any organization: corporations, non-profits, trade associations, and many other kinds of groups: any organization that may need someone to advocate on their behalf could use a lobbyist.

- It is best to be proactive and hire an in-house lobbyist before your organization encounters a severe problem. If you wait until a bill can significantly affect your business, and you have not been working all along to build connections with lawmakers, you probably will not have very much success in having your views considered.

CHAPTER 3
Associations

*"The achievements of an organization are the results of the
combined effort of each individual."*

Vince Lombardi,
Football Coach for the Green Bay Packers

SSOCIATIONS EXIST FOR practically everything, including an
association for associations.

As a business owner, the last thing you need is another job.

A business is influenced by outside factors such as legislation and regulation, and these can directly impact your bottom line. If you are currently a member of an association, or you have been in the past, then you are probably aware of the benefits that your association provides. An association can help with advocacy, public relations, and even with purchasing insurance.

In return for these benefits, members pay dues and volunteer to assist with tasks. These are great benefits, but for any organization—big or small—to make a difference, they must begin to think about how they can be an influencer in their given trade.

You may have heard it said that information is power.

Information is not exactly power, but—without it—your organization will never become influential. Associations are very common in both state and federal governments.

Just look at the National Bankers Association or the National Medical Association, and you can easily see the value of information. These are the experts in their fields.

Bankers are able to provide a vital perspective on banking regulations, and doctors are a credible group to turn to if a lawmaker is looking for advice on a health care bill. Data that supports your message is critical. Going to a legislator's office without information is a non-starter.

Don't speak from your feelings; speak from the facts. In the end, sound facts will win the day.

It is important to position yourself as an expert in your field.

If you have ever gone into a retailer and found that the salespeople didn't know any more than you, then you've already seen the value of expertise firsthand. Especially when it comes to businesses that deal with complex products or infrastructure, people will pay extra for your expert knowledge.

The same is also true for associations. Instead of trying to sell a service, you are trying to sell your position as an influencer.

Three key ingredients are necessary to becoming an authority in your field:

- **Understanding**

- **Collaborating**

- **Advising**

UNDERSTANDING

In the book, *The 7 Habits of Highly Effective People* by Dr. Stephen Covey, we pay particular attention to Habit 5: Seek First to Understand, Then to be Understood.

The main principle at play is that people are concerned more about what they have to say, rather than listening to the people or person they are talking to at that moment.

Through understanding, you can become a resource and an expert, and—as a result—you will stand out from the crowd. You begin to show understanding by providing information. This is one of the greatest tools at your disposal: helping others develop a greater understanding. Making your organization available to an agency or a legislative committee will allow you to become a trusted partner—and an expert.

The primary reason to provide information through your

organization's understanding is that it establishes your credibility. If you can go into a legislative office and talk not only with passion, but also with information to support your passion, you will be closer to victory.

Collaborating

Aside from understanding, you need to become familiar with one more tool if you want your association to take on an advisement role: collaboration.

More specifically, associations should consider coalition collaboration. Coalitions can make small associations seem larger, and they help to further a cause or discussion.

When I worked for Sunoco, I heard that all the time. Whether I was in Austin, Oklahoma City, or Harrisburg, lobbyists would say we are a "coalition town." The reason why alliances are formed across the nation, and why people take such pride in them, is because there is strength in an alliance.

Lawmakers need to know the issue is bigger than just one organization, and that the issue impacts people throughout their districts and the state.

Advising

Elected officials are interested in learning about your business. It's their job to get to know their constituents and understand the issues that impact those constituents. A business owner creates jobs, pays taxes, and contributes to the community. Therefore, elected officials have a vested interest in a business owner's success or failure.

If an executive director of an organization gives testimony on an issue, it often gets little reaction. However, if a business owner were to speak on the same issue to legislators from their region of the state, they would tend to be all ears.

Being a part of the process on some level will help build the foundation of a successful association. Even for small associations, involvement and relationships will provide access and open doors. Successful associations make the development of strong and meaningful relationships with elected officials a top priority. However, this success must come from members.

Members who are willing to take a few minutes to write or call their elected officials, to express their opinions regarding issues, are more likely to be heard. Even just one note or phone call can reap huge dividends. Reaching out to your elected officials and explaining to them how a piece of legislation might directly impact your business is a big game-changer.

In Pennsylvania, school property tax reform is a huge issue—and has been for more than forty years.

Within the past decade, a group of legislators has tried to push bills that would eliminate all school property taxes and replace them with higher sales and income taxes. Part of that proposal removes some exemptions to the sales tax, of which Pennsylvania has many, including clothing, food, necessities, and several services.

As you can imagine, this legislation is wildly popular with homeowners, especially senior citizens, many of whom cannot afford the skyrocketing property taxes in their part of the state. In fact, this concept is supported by a rather large group of very vocal taxpayers and their grassroots citizen taxpayer organizations.

Some would say that these groups have some of the best advocates: homeowners who have been forced to sell their homes because they cannot afford their property taxes. These groups have relied on their collective emotion to drive the change they're seeking. They have pressured lawmakers to support the plan, even pointing to the governor as being supportive.

On the other hand, this legislation is not popular with any organization whose services or products are currently exempt from the sales tax. Many of these groups have banded together in their coalition to fight this proposal. They have relayed scenarios of how their businesses would be impacted, how the state would ultimately lose revenue, and how the numbers just don't work.

This coalition has been successful, because—at the time of this writing—the legislation has not passed a single chamber of the General Assembly. In fact, the bill was defeated in the State Senate by a single, tie-breaking vote from the lieutenant governor.

These are all the different ways in which an association can benefit you. Whatever your trade, consider finding an association to join.

Associations can help you forge connections and network, and they can also help you band together with other compatible people. This is especially helpful if your business is small. With an association, you can pool your resources and approach lawmakers with a united front. When they see the size and scope of your association, legislators will know that they are dealing with a serious issue, and they will be receptive to your facts. They will welcome a chance to be further educated on the issue by a credible association that has been proven to be an expert in the industry.

SMALL ASSOCIATIONS

I often hear from small associations, "How can we compete? We are beaten before we try."

Before you decide to give up, please consider some areas of growth. Like when building a house, a strong foundation is critical to building a strong association—one that will stand over time and meet challenges head-on.

The following strategies can help:

- Form Connections

  Connection with the legislator as a constituent—and a part of your association—will reinforce that relationship. A great example is non-profits such as the March of Dimes or the American Heart Association. These organizations work primarily with volunteers, and they operate without PACs.

  So, how do they accomplish their goals?

  They do it by reaching out to legislators through their volunteers and forming a connection.

- Become an Expert

    How often have you gone to a big retailer and found sales-people with no more knowledge than you?

    Particularly for businesses that deal in complex products, people will pay extra for your expert knowledge. The same applies to an association, only here the customer is the Legislature. By becoming a resource and an expert, you will stand out from the crowd.

- Create a PAC Program

    If you don't have a PAC, start one.

    You need a PAC to get your message out, and it can help expand and attract new members. In addition to a website, consider developing a PAC program from nuts to bolts, including hosting regular events. Advertising is about repetition; it helps to get out your message.

    This is not a short-term fix; it's not timing. PACs are built over time, but once everyone buys into the idea and sees the connection, a PAC becomes a part of the association and not just something you offer members.

- Develop Coalitions

    Coalitions can make small associations seem larger, and they help to further a cause or discussion.

    Why?

    Because there is strength in alliances. Lawmakers need to know the issue is bigger than just one organization and that the issue impacts people throughout their district and the state.

    You can see the value of a coalition when we look at business issues. Creating an alliance with all the business groups shows lawmakers an issue is impactful. If you take an alliance and support it with real numbers, like job growth, you will reinforce impact and show value.

- Become a Part of the Process

Don't focus on how much money the PAC makes or how many issues you fight, but rather concentrate on the value the association provides the membership. The key to the success of any organization is the level of member involvement. Being a part of the process on some level will help build the foundation of a successful association.

When a small association tries to compete with a larger one, it may seem like you are fighting an army using sticks and rocks. If managed correctly, a small association can make a big difference.

KEY TAKEAWAYS

- There are all kinds of different associations. Whether you are a small or a large business, you can find an association of other like-minded people in your industry. Band together with them.

- Associations offer many benefits to members, in exchange for fees.

- To become an advisor, you must focus on three key areas:

  o Understanding

  o Collaborating

  o Advising

CHAPTER 4
Increasing Membership

"People don't buy what you do; they buy why you do it."

Simon Sinek, Author
and Motivational Speaker

IN THE BOOK, *Start with Why, How Great Leaders Inspire Everyone to Take Action*, Simon Sinek points to the need to focus on the "why." This is one word I learned early on as a child; just ask my wife.

It is probably the major question a membership organization should be asking when developing its government affairs or public affairs program. Far too often, an organization forgets why they are doing what they are doing. "Why" is very important and helps guide an association to its overall goal.

Simon goes on to say in his book that developing a "why" will lead you to passion.

If any organization is to succeed, that organization must remain passionate. More than a mission statement, your organization must clearly define your purpose, which is the basis of passion. This is not measured by dollar signs or membership—although cash flow is important. Purpose is the driving force behind your program. If the purpose is defined and supported by passion, the rest will take care of itself.

Attracting new members, along with retaining existing members in an organization, needs to be approached with specific strategies. The main issue is the ability to engage someone and show them the value of membership.

This value may come in the form of publications, continuing education opportunities, certifications, and group insurance. It could also come in the form of networking opportunities, such as interactions within the association or conferences and events.

Purpose

If you have a world-class athlete who has no purpose, you will not have a world-class athlete for long.

I am a huge fan of the NBA and Cleveland Cavaliers superstar Lebron James, and I even followed his victories on the court when he was in high school.

From the start of his career, commentators would say that moving from high school to the NBA could be a real issue, but no one measured his heart.

True, he is not perfect, and going to Miami was not a high point in his career, but no one can ever question his purpose. He says openly that he wants to be a role model and has set his focus on "greatness." One cannot achieve greatness by just showing up for work; they must set a purpose that takes an organization to the next level.

Increasing your membership is important, but it's not worth anything if you can't keep those members. To maintain your numbers, it's equally important to keep existing members happy. New members are at the greatest risk for drop-off. This is because they are still getting acclimated to the organization and deciding if it is for them. They are almost like new employees who need the onboarding process.

During the first few months of their membership, new members will be inspecting and analyzing each interaction they have with the organization—or they will be examining the lack of communication. It is important to use this unofficial probationary period as a time to reinforce the organization's value and to begin to deliver on that promise of value. For these members, reach out to them at events, through direct mail or via social media. The medium doesn't matter so much if you are staying in regular communication.

Next, market to your members. Use social media to your advantage. Ensure that your organization has a presence across several different platforms. That doesn't mean you should sign your organization up for an account with every single social media outlet there is. There are far too many: Facebook, Twitter, Tumbler, Wattpad, Redditt, StumbleUpon, Pinterest, YouTube, Quora, Snapchat, Instagram, Google+, Quotes, DeviantArt, and LinkedIn. There are much more than even these. This is a just a list of some of the most-used social media platforms.

If you sign up for every single one of these social media platforms, you will not have enough time to devote to all of them. Your presence will inevitably be weak on some of them. It is better not to be on a social media site than to have an account and never use it or post anything. People will follow you for the same reason that they have joined your organization: a perceived value.

When people browse the internet, deciding what they will devote their attention to, they are looking for something valuable to them: this could be information, entertainment, networking, or money-saving opportunities. If they follow you, they are doing so in the hopes of exchanging their attention for value. If they provide you with their attention and never receive anything for it, they will feel cheated. This will hurt your brand and reputation.

Instead of spreading yourself too thinly, try to do a bit of market research and figure out which sites your members use.

Where do the majority of your members spend their time online?

If your members tend to be middle-aged or older, there is a good chance that they use Facebook for their social media interactions. College-aged young professionals tend to be partial to Twitter, LinkedIn, Snapchat, and Instagram. Women tend to enjoy Pinterest more than men do. All ages and genders enjoy YouTube, while hardly anyone uses Google+. These are some of the things to consider when choosing where to focus your online marketing efforts.

An association of young women in business might choose to utilize Twitter and Pinterest. An association for retired individuals might decide to focus their efforts on Facebook and YouTube.

You could also conduct a survey of your members, rather than relying on statistics. Sometimes these are not entirely accurate, or there may be members of your organization who are outliers and use social media differently than you might assume.

Once you have decided where to focus your online efforts, a social media marketing campaign can be an excellent way to build your brand and keep members engaged. It can also be a fun and inviting way to attract new members and let the world know what your organization is all about. There are many ways to orchestrate a social media campaign. It's all about creativity and generating excitement.

The best social media campaigns get people involved. It shouldn't just be about generating content to be viewed passively. You need to find ways to inspire members to get up and do something. A water-sustainability non-profit in Boston ran a very successful social media campaign to generate excitement around its water-bottle filling stations. The non-profit found that the majority of its audience was students (its water-bottle filling stations were primarily situated on college campuses), so the organization spent most of their social media time on Instagram.

The group put a counter on each water-bottle filling station that announced to the user how many bottles of water had been filled. When the ticker reached 10,000, users were challenged to take a picture of themselves filling their bottle and post it to Instagram.

The non-profit sent prizes to everyone who did this, and it was able to create a large degree of excitement around its brand—and around water-sustainability issues in general. The social media campaign gave the organization a launching point to talk about how easy it is to make the switch and do away with plastic bottles altogether, thus ceasing to contribute to the North Pacific Garbage Patch in the ocean. The campaign also increased the group's brand recognition, got more people to start using the water-bottle filling stations, and educated students on the importance of staying hydrated.

This is just one example of a very successful and creative social media campaign. Employ some original thinking and intuition, and you can create one for your organization as well.

A trade magazine is another great resource, and it can be used to advertise to new members. A trade magazine can be used as a way to let potential members know everything that your organization is all about. You can use this tool to encourage them to join and fight for the issues that matter most to them.

In the case of entrepreneurs, the issue that would matter the most to them is their business. Advertisements or submitted articles in those trade publications can focus on what your organization is fighting for in each state, emphasizing how you can help with their state's specific needs.

Currently, I write an article each month for a magazine produced by one of my clients, and I use this opportunity to discuss a current legislative issue, to talk about political trends, and to break down election results. This content provides value to the client and, in turn, to its members. I have also found the article to be especially helpful at the client's networking events. Because my photo is included, association members have introduced themselves to me and mentioned they've read my articles. This often leads to a discussion about my role in their association and what I offer to them, yet again emphasizing the value of their membership.

Another way to garner interest is by sponsoring professional events, which associations are often known for, whether they include an annual dinner, a quarterly lunch, or online professional-learning webinars. You can recruit new members by allowing attendees to bring a friend or guest.

A way to do this is to obtain member-to-member sponsors. Develop an annual membership drive, and reward those who generate the highest number of new members with a membership discount. This is a way to generate word-of-mouth advertising. You are also likely to get new members who are a good fit for your organization. If they are friends or colleagues with existing members, then it is probable that they have the same interests and needs.

It may also be beneficial to enact regional advisory boards or member meetings. By asking your current members for their opinions, you'll be able to adjust your membership benefits to appeal to them. You may find out that your members would enjoy a benefit that would be very easy to offer. Then you could provide them with tremendous value—with little additional effort.

You can also create an annual member survey to collect feedback. If you are trying to choose between several different, new benefits to offer members, you could create a questionnaire to ascertain which of them will be most valuable to your members.

Buy-in for these types of benefits also reaps the rewards, in that people generally like being included in a decision.

And the happier they are, the more likely they will stay members.

You could sponsor a day at the Capitol for members.

This type of event would deliver considerable value to them. It is not important how many members attend. What is important is showing all your members, both those who can attend and those who can't, that your organization is working for them and fighting to make a difference. As part of this event, consider sponsoring a Legislator of the Year Award to create buzz in the Capitol and among your members.

The most important factor with these events is consistency. When you set up a monthly program, make sure that you stay with that program month after month. When you set something in place, it is like making a promise to your members.

In the case of an annual conference or event, you are giving them something to expect and look forward to. If you then decide to stop offering this event, you may disappoint your members, and your organization will appear flaky and unreliable.

A primary purpose of your organization is to gather together like-minded people for networking and creating change. By engaging with the community and using social media, events, conferences, and online learning tools to get your name in front of people, you can build a member base that is energized and excited about a common cause.

And that helps your ability to influence change.

ASSOCIATIONS

When my job was eliminated at an energy company, I wanted to build a trade association, like the organizations I belonged to in Texas and Oklahoma. It seemed easy enough, as I had all the right contacts.

First, I reached out to all the people I knew in Texas to get a blueprint for the structure of an organization to help with forming the non-profit.

Next, I contacted a web designer to help me put it on paper, so I could show companies and take the intangible and make it tangible.

Finally, I reached out to companies, people, and lobbyists about building the organization.

Getting the blueprint for the organization and designing the website went quickly. In a matter of three months, I had a website, a logo, and an organizational structure.

This being in place, I started reaching out to lobbyists I knew who represented energy companies, and many were very anxious to be involved. At the same time, I contacted law firms about bringing their clients into the organization, and they were very interested too.

My next step was contacting companies and putting the pins in place for the trade association—but this is where the idea became a passing dream. Companies did not see the need to organize and build a membership organization. They felt they were covered by the groups already in place.

This was a rather expensive teachable moment, but it really helped to see some of the key takeaways in building any associations.

- Always Focus on the Need

    People make decisions based on fear and hope. An organization or corporation thinks about government affairs and public affairs because they see the need. Creating this association before there was a need made it hard to convince companies to join the organization.

The demand must be authentic and organic, or—in the end—the organization will never grow.

- Start Out Small and Build from the Ground Up

  Rome was not built in a day, and I think this applies to growing an association too. Some of the best and most significant associations I have seen were built one brick at a time.

- Websites and Social Media are Tools

  A website and social media participation are great tools to validate your organization, like a business card. But a website will never grow a business or organization alone.

- You Need an Anchor Store to Build a Mall

  When I worked in retail, managers would talk about the necessity of an anchor store like a Macy's, Dick's Sporting Goods, or Neiman Marcus to draw in customers. This could not be truer for an association.

  Anchor stores or large corporations bring in other members. As the saying goes, "The only job you can start at the top is that of digging a hole."

KEY TAKEAWAYS

- It is essential for an association to focus both on increasing membership and providing value to existing members.

- If you have a world-class athlete who has no purpose, you will not have a world-class athlete for long.

- Goals are the driving force behind your program. If the purpose is defined, the rest will take care of itself.

- Some of the ways that you can provide value to your members are via conferences and other networking opportunities, as well as online learning webinars.

- Use social media strategically and focus on the social media platforms where most of your members can be found.

- Market to members via emails, events, and creative social media campaigns.

- When using social media, try to encourage involvement.

- Generate new membership by offering incentives for existing members who recommend people.

CHAPTER 5
Political Action Committees

"Research shows that the climate of an organization influences an individual's contribution far more than the individual himself."

W. Edwards Deming,
Management Thinker

D URING EVERY PRESIDENTIAL election cycle, we hear about the need to uplift the middle class or get tough on Wall Street. Obviously, these issues are good politics and have been the cornerstone of elections, but is this what really matters—or is it the money?

Many will argue our political system is broken. So, to begin, let's look at the Pennsylvania General Assembly as if it had layers, like an onion. The first layer is that Pennsylvania's Legislature is bicameral, and that—in and of itself—is a significant barrier to legislative action.

Our next layer is a House and Senate controlled by almost veto-proof Republican majorities.

Moreover, when these chambers are more conservatively idealistic, that adds another layer to our onion. These layers mean that whatever legislation is passed must have a broad public consensus from staunchly conservative members to take a specific course of action.

When the consensus is not wide enough, the legislative process grinds to a halt, and we are left with tears in our eyes, much like what an onion does.

A recent analysis of state disclosures and television advertising showed that spending in a seven-way race for seats on the Pennsylvania Supreme Court eclipsed $15.8 million, making it the most expensive judicial election in US history.

The narrative that money can't buy elections may be true, with races closer to the voter, like for State House or Senate seats. Often, when money looks like it is a factor, you will find that money did not buy the election—but it did help to push an issue that got someone elected.

Now, a variety of reasons exist for why the better-financed candidates are victorious more often and, conversely, why winning candidates are often better financed.

One huge advantage is incumbency. Those who have won elections in the past begin any race with the benefit of having already built fundraising networks. On average, they have more than double the amount of money brought in by their challengers and a re-election rate of nearly ninety percent.

Also, some would argue that, in many cases, the candidates who win the most votes do so based on the same electability, popularity, and qualifications that make them the best at fundraising—and vice versa.

A candidate who is compelling enough to get you to open your wallet should, in theory, also be able to get you to head to the ballot box for him or her. Over the past fifty-plus years now, since the national pollster Gallup predicted the 1960 Kennedy-Nixon presidential election, pollsters and pundits have tried to predict the outcomes, like casinos bet on horses.

The difference is the odds are stacked even higher against predicting an election when the main variable is voting. Marketing a campaign is like paying for advertising in a business: Name recognition will get the customer to the door, but reputation and value keep them coming back. One without the other will make it difficult to grow your business or, in this case, voters' confidence and continual support for a candidate.

If you don't have a political action committee (PAC), start one.

You need a PAC to get your message out, and a PAC can help expand and attract new members. A PAC is a tool used by an association to pool their money and resources. This money can be used to support specific candidates or to run advertising campaigns.

PACs are built over time, but once everyone buys into the idea and sees the connection, it becomes a part of the association and not just something offered to members.

The primary reason for forming a PAC is to help elect candidates with views that align with your organization.

You want to see people in office who believe in your issues and those who have actively championed your opinions in the past. You may also want to support candidates who are new to the process but understand and agree with your goals. Political action committees first came into being as a result of Watergate, when there were few rules concerning how money was spent by corporations. Since that time, we have seen the growth of state PAC programs and federal programs, and now super PACs. Regardless of the PAC type, without money, a PAC makes little difference.

It's important to remember that an active PAC requires buy-in from within the organization, from the top down. A corporation requires a buy-in from the president, and an association needs the board of directors.

Without buy-in from either, the PAC will not survive.

During my days at Sunoco, I played a considerable role in the company's PAC and traveled across the country, encouraging its employees to donate to it. I gave presentations on how and why the company's PAC was valuable and even brought in some key policy-makers and company executives to show them the value of their contributions.

At another association where I worked, I further developed and organized its PAC to ensure that contributions were being directed to the right candidates and office-holders. And when it came time to disperse those PAC funds, I tried to attend as many political fundraisers as I could.

A check is a useful tool, but it's always wise to have a face to your organization—and I wanted that face to be mine.

After all, if the elected official had a question about how a specific policy might impact my association or business, I wanted them to contact me. And if I was unable to attend the fundraiser, I would schedule a time and place to personally deliver the check. Doing so gives you an even better opportunity to meet up with the officials personally, and they are more likely to remember you, rather than everyone present at the fundraiser. Also, I was always mindful of campaign laws in various states. In Pennsylvania, one cannot mix legislative business with political work, so it is illegal to give PAC checks in a legislative office.

What makes a PAC so effective?

The United States Supreme Court has ruled that money is speech. Donating to a PAC shows that your members have a voice. Giving a PAC check unifies that voice on behalf of your organization.

That voice has power.

Building a PAC will help you to build relationships with lawmakers who share your vision and understand your issues.

I am sure you have asked yourself many times:

- How did this regulation become policy?

- Or how did this law get passed?

During the process of reviewing legislation, it is important to have legislators engaged who have your back. Otherwise, you might find a law or regulation was passed that you did not see coming. Bad laws and weak policies happen when people and organizations are not engaged in the process.

The size of a PAC does matter, but there are limits to how much a PAC can do. This is because strict laws govern how PACs can spend their money and how much they can contribute to candidates each election cycle.

Still, a PAC is a valuable tool, and it's one you should employ to get the most out of your advocacy efforts. Don't focus on how much money it makes or how many issues you fight; rather focus on the value of the association that has the PAC.

IMPORTANT POINTS TO CONSIDER WHEN BUILDING A PAC:

- Decide if you want a federal or state PAC.

- Read the law: state and federal PACs are regulated, and you need to know the law.

- DO NOT pick a treasurer from the board of directors. This position has complete fiduciary responsibility and will be held personally responsible for all activities in the PAC.

- Keep accurate records for your files and for reporting purposes.

- Purchase the proper technology, like QuickBooks or Aristotle, as a way to help document and retain accurate files.

And always remember that contributing to a PAC and directing resources to a specific candidate or elected official is not a guarantee of the outcome you want.

A PAC merely gives you greater access and your chance to be heard. The elected official still makes the final decision.

Too many people—donors and candidates—have gone to prison over the years by making promises with PAC checks.

KEY TAKEAWAYS

- A political action committee (PAC) is a valuable tool that associations can employ. A PAC allows associations to pool money and influence.

- A PAC can be used to contribute money to candidates, although laws regulate how that money can be spent and how much can be given each election cycle.

- A PAC can be used to run advertising campaigns. These may be in favor of, or against, specific candidates, or they may revolve around a single issue, such as gun control or tax policy.

- A PAC requires buy-ins from within the organization.

CHAPTER 6
Not All Policies Are Good Policies

"Young people have so much more power than they tend to think to be able to affect politics. And if people will organize and get involved and go out and knock on doors and hand out leaflets and make a change, then they can determine the future."

John F. Kennedy,
Thirty-Fifth President of the United States

REGULATION AND LEGISLATION have a direct impact on business, but business professionals do not always comprehend the difficulties of adequately funding government programs, and politicians do not always understand the complexities of running a business.

So, educating both about the potential effects regulation or legislation could have on an industry is critical to the success or failure of government affairs.

Many times, when I was working with the National Federation of Independent Business (NFIB), we would poll our members and find that taxes and regulations were the two biggest issues impacting small businesses.

We often hear candidates say that they are the allies of small business, but then they get elected and their actions don't always seem to support these sentiments.

But we hold them accountable.

Every two years, NFIB compiles a report card on specific issues it championed or fought against—such as liquor privatization or lowering the Corporate Net Income Tax—and ranked members on their votes. This was a time-consuming effort, especially considering the size of the Pennsylvania General Assembly and its 203-member House and 50-member Senate. But the work paid off. Those who voted with our organization on the main issues were given a Guardian of Small Business Award, and those with a 100-percent score on our issues were selected for an even more prestigious honor.

We recognized those members with certificates and photos, which many of the Guardians of Small Business then sent to their local newspapers or posted to their websites and social media accounts. Not only did this help the legislator, but it also increased our name recognition as being the voice of small business.

That was the value of helping legislators who supported good policies.

But sometimes, bad policies happen when no one is noticing.

For example, let's look at the increase of title and lien fees in Pennsylvania.

While raising revenue to fix roads and repair structurally deficient bridges, the General Assembly, along with the governor at the time, Tom Corbett, not only increased the state's gasoline tax but also sought to implement or improve a whole host of other fees: driver license and registration fees and those on vehicles titles and liens.

Make no mistake: this "fee increase" was just another word for a tax.

And that tax added quite a financial burden, not only to those who purchase cars but those who sell cars for a living, including one of my clients, the Pennsylvania Independent Automobile Dealers Association (PIADA).

If you were to ask PIADA members, you would have found that most of them saw the need to rebuild the infrastructure, because they traveled those same roads and bridges every day and were willing to pay their fair share.

But was that really their "fair" share?

Increasing fees by as much as 300 percent made this look less like a fee and more like a tax on independent auto dealers. This fee put the funding of transportation projects on the backs of small businesses that could not take the losses that a larger company could. Small businesses don't have that sort of money accounted for in their budgets the way larger businesses do: a large business might account for large fees, considering it the cost of doing business.

However, for a small business, a fee increase at this level would force employers to look for ways to internally cut costs. This could mean cutting salaries or employee hours or offering smaller benefits packages to employees. A business may even end up relocating to another state to avoid these hefty fees. This leads to a loss of jobs in the geographic area.

But, in the end, it is about the survival of a business: a business must do what it can to stay afloat.

And that is why a lobbyist is valuable.

Government officials need to realize that businesses operate on profits and losses. If costs of doing business are increased, they will seek other ways to cut expenses. This might even mean looking for a tax strategy that can help them save money. It often means operating in states that are friendlier to business. If an increase is only going to drive business out of a state, then it really defeats its purpose. The state won't have an increase in revenue if it's driving business away, thus leading to fewer businesses available to pay taxes or increased fees.

The answer is that there needs to be more of a dialogue between government and business. If a program is written without considering the consequences, then it is just a solution chasing a problem.

The government officials who wrote these programs were not trying to hurt small businesses.

Why would they want to do that?

It just wouldn't make any sense for them. Elected officials want to see businesses in their state do well. They want their state's economy to thrive, and they want to see continual job growth. When small businesses and entrepreneurs do well, the entire state does well. A strong economy makes a strong state—and it is a telling mark of success for those in office.

The reason why these same officials wrote those programs into effect is simply because they didn't understand the disproportionally negative impact that the fees would have on small businesses.

They believed the costs would be passed along to the customer and included as part of a far larger purchase—that of a vehicle—and might be included as part of the financing. When a car payment is $300 or $305, people don't notice the $5 difference.

But the costs aren't passed along. This is where advocacy was needed on behalf of the small business owners. It's a lobbyist's job to intervene in matters such as these.

How could a lobbyist have helped?

He might have gotten in touch with one of his contacts and asked for a meeting to discuss the fee changes, where he would have brought some evidence to support his client's position. He might have referenced a similar situation in the past, or in other states, where small businesses suffered from exorbitant fees. Then he might have explained how the prices would affect the businesses and some of the measures that the business owners would have been forced to take.

Finally, he would have made some suggestions that would satisfy both parties.

In this case, the elected officials were looking for ways to raise money for infrastructure, and the small business owners wanted to be able to stay in business without relocating or cutting back on salaries or employee benefits. The solution would have to be one that met both needs.

As we discussed earlier, a raise in taxes might be a better solution than such massive fees. A lobbyist might suggest this, and then explain his reasons why this solution would be a better alternative.

KEY TAKEAWAYS

- Some policies can hurt business. Communication between businesses and lawmakers is essential so that these bad policies are not enacted.

- If a policy hurts a business too much, the business may need to cut back on benefits to employees—or even move the business to another geographic location. Businesses always need to make up the money somehow.

- The best solution is one in which both parties walk away happy.

CHAPTER 7
Lobbying In Public Affairs
And Government Affairs

"An organization's ability to learn, and translate that learning into action rapidly, is the ultimate competitive advantage."

Jack Welch,
Former Chairman and CEO of General Electric

LOBBYISTS HAVE TWO primary roles: to influence public opinion and to guide policy.

When lobbyists strive to impact public opinion, they are involved in public affairs.

When lobbyists seek to educate legislators and sway policy, they are involved in government affairs. [6]

A lobbyist may become involved in public affairs via community outreach; this is done in several different ways. It could involve

---

6 Wesolowski, Hannah. "Lobbying and Political Involvement FAQs." Public Affairs Council. Pac.org. Web. 22 Feb. 2017.

attending meetings and panels, speaking at various events, or advertising campaigns.

Advertising campaigns are often funded by PACs. These campaigns can be specific to an issue or may be in support of a candidate.

The National Rifle Association may run ads attempting to educate the public on matters of gun ownership and any legislation coming up that may impact gun owner's rights.

The World Wildlife Foundation may run ads to spread the word about conservation efforts or the endangerment status of different species.

A lobbyist becomes involved in government affairs when they directly attempt to educate or persuade lawmakers. They may meet with various legislators and form relationships. They may speak at congressional or legislative hearings or panels, presenting their facts and shining a light on the way a piece of legislation may affect a business or organization. They may use PAC funds to contribute to the campaigns of candidates who agree with their positions.

Lobbyists may even review a piece of legislation and suggest changes. When lobbyists do this, they are engaging in legislative affairs, which is similar to national outreach. Sometimes a lobbyist may even draft the suggested changes, and if enough legislators agree with them, they may be written into the final bill.

At its core, government affairs focuses on communication and building relationships. Education is a vital part of this process, including helping elected officials to understand their constituent's concerns. Lobbyists aim to educate lawmakers on the potential consequences of different pieces of legislation.

Regulation and legislation have a direct impact on businesses, but business professionals do not always comprehend the difficulties of adequately funding government programs, and politicians do not always understand the complexities of running a business.

So, educating both about the potential effects that a regulation or legislation could have on an industry is critical. If each party knows a bit more about the struggles faced by the other, compromise and accommodation become more feasible.

Naturally, lobbying can influence the law, and it really requires two things: contacts and knowledge of the system of government. Without an understanding of the law-making process, opportunities to shape the outcome of legislation can be limited.

Government affairs is about developing long-term relationships with officials, so that they can understand our priorities and we can understand theirs. Like any business relationship, they need to be cultivated, cared for, and communicated with on a regular basis.

When considering the best lobbyist for your organization, you need to think about the legislative aspect. The political party with the majority in the respective legislative chamber sets the agenda, and that is critical to how you manage the issues.

While working for a major national corporation, I was faced with this question:

Do I keep a lobbyist who was not connected to the majority party but had been with the corporation for a long time and had developed some local contacts attached to the corporation?

As you review your lobbyists, it is important to see how they fit with members.

- Are they liked?

- Are they getting things done?

- Do they have a good reputation?

- Are they honest?

- If they are out there, are they representing your interests?

That is why you must talk to legislators. The expression that "This is not personal, it's business," applies.

In doing my due diligence in and around the Capitol in that particular state, it was apparent the lack of relationships between my hired lobbyist and the majority in power was, in fact, hurting our legislative relationships. While it was a hard decision to make, I decided it was in our best interest to take a different path and choose someone else to represent us.

It doesn't do any good if you are only reaching out to contacts when you need something. Throughout this book, I continually emphasize that you shouldn't just be contacting legislators when a relevant bill is coming up. People can see right through this, and they will feel as though they are being used. Building and developing relationships should be a long-term goal of your organization.

It's true that when you network, you are probably trying to get something out of it. In this case, you seek to get some pull and influence in the legislative process. But that doesn't mean that you should only connect with people when you want to get something out of it. You should connect with people genuinely and get to know them.

You will have a tough time building relationships if you aren't genuine about it.

To be genuine, you should make a real and concentrated effort to get to know people. Care about them and be helpful when you can. Assist other people when they need it and trust that it will come back to you at some point.

Shake hands, remember names, and look people in the eye. People appreciate this. These are all small gestures, but they will have vast real-life applications. Any government affairs or public policy program starts with good organizational design and structure. The key is to stay closely integrated with those with whom you do business and interact. Share and refer clients and contacts.

If this happens, both can grow and be successful.

THREE PRIMARY COMPONENTS OF GOVERNMENT AFFAIRS/ PUBLIC POLICY

- **Structure**

    No matter the name of the group ("public affairs" and "government affairs" are common choices), top companies make sure that these organizations excel at analysis and stakeholder engagement, not just at lobbying and industry-group participation.

Regardless of how the government affairs function may be structured, engagement with high-level stakeholders is a CEO-level concern, so having the high-level government affairs project leader report to the chief executive is critical.

Special note: Some law firms combine the law practice with the lobbying practice, and some make them separate. The trend is to separate and form policy groups, because conflicts have arisen with hourly billing for services for a law firm and not with lobbying. If part of a law firm, the key is to stay closely integrated with the law end and share and refer clients back and forth. If this happens, they can both grow and be successful.

- **Collaboration**

  The ability to convene and collaborate across functions is vital for success. When units aren't viewed as good partners, they can't help the businesses to engage with regulators, coordinate the development of positions proactively, and monitor issues—both legislative and regulatory.

  Lack of internal communication can create struggles that can mean a lost opportunity if, for example, a firm is late on a legal or regulatory issue. This gives a perception of not being engaged or involved, and that can cause many clients to consider alternatives.

- **Talent** - Once the external affairs group structure has been determined, the next step is: How should it be staffed? And how should it collaborate with other functions? The next task is staffing it with good people. Choose from: **industry-specific** or **high-profile lobbyists and former politicians** who bring credibility and clout.

Any type can work well, so long as the leader coordinates effectively across business units while getting—and keeping—the respect and attention of senior management.

Not all lobbyists are equal.

If one were to stand in any state Capitol during a legislative session, you would see lobbyists standing in the rotunda or outside the chambers, waiting to catch a legislator or staff member between meetings.

Typically, one would hear the words, "What are you hearing?" or "What do you know?" They are always asking to get the inside tip that they can report back or to hear the latest first—an asset for which their clients, companies, or associations are paying good money.

I am sure you have heard or were taught that knowledge is power, and—in lobbying—that is true. The only issue is that knowledge without access means nothing. Graduating from law school at the top of your class without a job at a law firm or having paying clients just means you have a costly picture frame on the wall.

At the beginning of this book, we talked about public affairs and government affairs. Both are interrelated with lobbying, but both have a different outcome and approach. In this chapter, I want to talk about public affairs and what that can mean to your organization.

I am sure you have seen the words "public affairs" somewhere and wondered what the distinction between public affairs and government affairs is.

Chart of Public Affairs

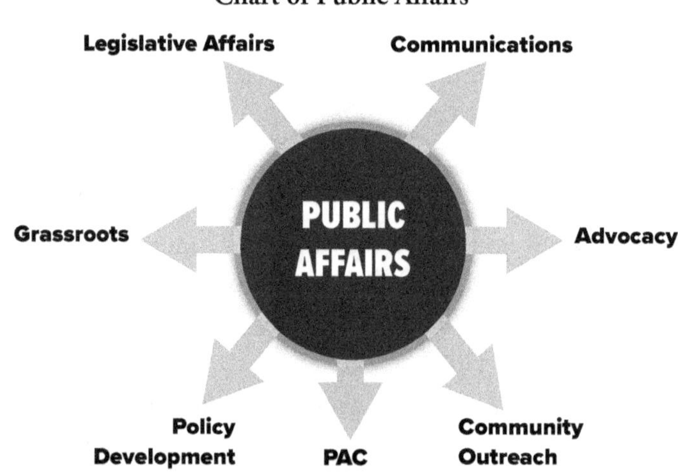

Public affairs is focused primarily on communication with the public through communications and community outreach. Organizations like an institute or forum will focus on policy development. The primary goal of this organization is to educate. A goal of a corporate lobbyist is to educate and lobby specific issues. Such may be the case of a state chamber lobbying against a tax increase or an energy association lobbying against regulations.

Frankly, where you stand or how you view lobbying is really the overriding issue.

If you believe lobbying is about influence peddling, then you are probably opposed, but if you see the lobbyist as someone who can provide access to help your organization show your value, then your perspective changes.

Yes, there are less than genuine operators who are independent contract lobbyists, but that can be applied to any profession.

Chart of Government Affairs

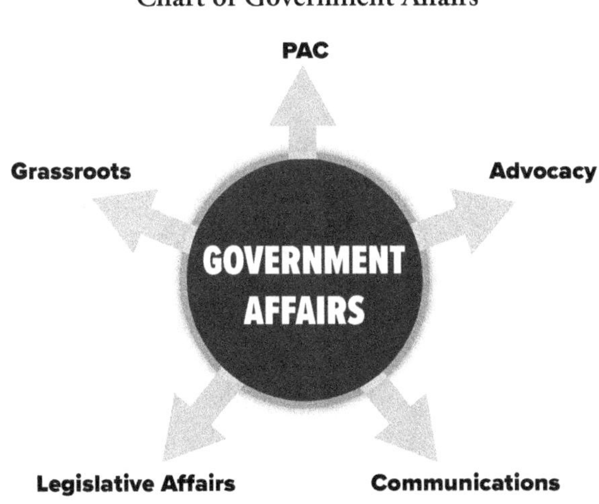

Government affairs primarily focuses on the organization's relationship with the legislators, committees, leadership, agencies, and the governor's office.

The main difference between public affairs and government affairs is that groups typically work with their membership only and do not reach out to the public.

They are smaller and take less time to manage and less cost to maintain. Smaller groups with limited budgets use this approach.

NON-PROFIT LOBBYING: GOVERNMENT AFFAIRS

Some people believe it's unethical for a lobbyist to work for a non-profit, because working for the greater good is noble and right.

This reference applies to securing funds for hospitals or school districts, even money for Boys and Girls Clubs or afterschool programs.

As a lobbyist, I have helped the American Heart Association, American Lung Association, the Boys and Girls Clubs, and the March of Dimes successfully lobby their issues in Pennsylvania.

For these groups, their purpose typically involves shining a light on a subject that needs attention, versus actual lobbying, as you would in a corporation or for a trade association. Although, if the effort requires a line item in the budget, these issues can be just as challenging.

COMMUNICATION

The world of business today has become very sophisticated. If you sell cars or work for an energy company or are involved in banking, you know what I am talking about. In the world of government, this growing trend means both businesses and associations need to allocate resources for someone who can help that group navigate the waters of government.

Operating as a guide, you will often find former government regulators working for large corporations in public affairs. Some lobbyists are hired as experts on a given issue like banking, insurance, health care, or energy.

Now more than ever, it is not enough just to hire an expert. The new level of sophisticated social media and integrated communication requires a strategy for how to communicate with stakeholders. This applies to those within a given community and across the country. In the world of public affairs, this person will need to be aware of the 24/7 news cycle, community and external relations, internal communications, and government affairs. These are all linked by the need to be consistent in message and to speak as one voice.

KEY TAKEAWAYS

- The two ways in which lobbyists can help an organization are via either public affairs or government affairs.

- Public affairs is the process by which lobbyists try to influence the opinion of the public. They may do this through community outreach or by implementing advertising campaigns.

- Government affairs is the process by which lobbyists try to influence lawmakers. They may do this by building relationships with legislators and educating them on different topics.

CHAPTER 8
Do Elections Matter?
Why Should I Care?

*"Nothing in all the world is more dangerous than sincere
ignorance and conscientious stupidity."*

Martin Luther King, Jr.,
Leader of the Civil Rights Movement

THE VERY FIRST time I was involved in politics was at a mock
Democratic National Convention at Westminster College in
New Wilmington, Pennsylvania.

Westminster is a Presbyterian-based liberal arts college, where I
majored in theater as a freshman. (Later, I switched to a history major,
although most people think theater and politics fit very nicely.)

Every four years, since 1936, except for the wartime year of 1944,
an extraordinary event has occurred at Westminster—the mock presidential nominating convention, one of the oldest events of its kind
that's found at only a handful of colleges and universities. During years
when the country's political parties hold their national conventions,

Westminster stages its mock convention for the party currently out of office.

I am a lifelong Republican, but I loved watching Jesse Jackson on TV, talking about hope and that no matter where you are from, you are somebody. As a boy who lost his father at age six, Jackson's words meant more to me than most, and—with that—I submitted my name to be his campaign manager for our convention.

Being excited about my role as Jesse Jackson's campaign manager at a Presbyterian college did not put me on the Christmas card lists of many people in the student body, but—as any twenty-one-year-old—I was determined to change the world.

I may not have changed the world with that mock convention, but what I was to experience changed me and how I saw that world.

Before I could be the campaign manager on campus for the Jesse Jackson for President Campaign, I had to apply for the post. The line of applicants was not long, but I was more than prepared—it was my time to talk about the Reverend Jackson. By the end of the meeting, everyone knew I was very serious—and my mission was to win.

My first phone call for the campaign was to his national office in Chicago, Illinois, and then I called Philadelphia, where someone directed me to a small town that is very close to where I grew up and not far from Westminster College. The town was Farrell, Pennsylvania, and his campaign manager was the Reverend Dr. Carrol M. Felton Jr., the minister of the Baptist Church in Farrell—no farther than five miles from my home and in the heart of what many considered the projects.

For me, it was home, and I did not see them as projects.

I called Dr. Felton from my dorm room, and he invited me to his house to talk about the campaign. I went there in a flash.

On a Saturday afternoon, I drove to meet Dr. Felton at his home. His wife answered the door and asked me to wait in the living room, and Dr. Felton would get me when he was ready.

I was terrified to meet this man—he had a Ph.D. in theological urbanization and sociology, and his books were everywhere I could see. When I went into the room, I sat down and immediately felt like I was with someone more than a campaign manager, but I could not put my finger on it.

That meeting lasted for over an hour, and then—the next day—he invited me to a rally with Reverend Jackson at the Youngstown, Ohio airport, which wasn't far away. I came to the event and was introduced as Reverend Keaton.

One minister said he did not know I was a reverend, and I replied, "It happened fast."

From the airport, we went to Dr. Felton's church, and I stood next to Reverend Jackson as part of the Rainbow Coalition. In fact, on the television news that night, I could be seen in the background.

About a week later, Reverend Felton asked me to attend a fundraiser for the campaign of Congresswoman Shirley Chisholm, who was the featured speaker. (She was from Brooklyn and ran for president in 1972. As a ten-year-old, I remember watching her run for president with my mother during the presidential campaign.) When the evening ended, Reverend Felton introduced me to her, and I had a hard time finding words—some people now would find that hard to believe.

Two weeks later was the Westminster convention. The convention began with parades followed by party platform discussions. On the second day of the convention, nomination speeches were given.

Our featured speaker was an up-and-coming Congressman from Delaware: Joe Biden. He gave a very rousing speech and energized the delegates at the convention. His remarks were made with the passion and sincerity that has become vintage Biden. (I recently found a picture of me with my Jesse Jackson T-shirt on, talking with Congressman Biden. Who knew then?)

While passionate, his remarks were not received well by all the delegates, although I believe these statements set the table for the Reverend Jackson to make a push for the nomination. More than anything, Congressman Biden validated our campaign message and that we should be given a second look.

Most nominating conventions up to this time had taken as many as thirteen ballots. On this night, Senator Gary Hart won the nomination on the fifth ballot, becoming the nominee with 717 votes. Jackson had 228, and Mondale had 84.

As a result, the vice-presidential nomination went to the Reverend Jesse Jackson.

I realized at this moment that elections matter and that, although a small snapshot of a bigger picture, this reflected how our democracy works.

Three or four days after the convention, I was in the library trying to catch up on my Central American journal for my history class, and while I was reading the *Wall Street Journal*, it all made sense.

See, Dr. Felton was a professor of Reverend Jackson's in 1964 at the Chicago Theological Seminary in Chicago. The article went on to talk about the event in Farrell and how they both worked on Operation Breadbasket together during the Civil Rights Movement of the 1960s. No wonder I felt what I did in the room when I met Dr. Felton.

I had been in the presence of greatness.

I can honestly say that I have never met anyone with Dr. Felton's presence. The last time I spoke with him, I told him the same, and he spoke with me about his family's struggles with civil rights in the Deep South. Sadly, after searching for him for several years, I found out he passed away.

If you had told me this would be the only lesson I would learn from college, I would pay for it again many times over.

In school, we learn that two plus two equals four, but in politics and in government, that is not the case. For many people, that perceived confusion is the very thing they dislike about elections and politics. They want straight answers, not life lessons.

As I watched the Republican and Democrat presidential candidate debates during the 2016 election, I was left wondering what happened.

Have things really changed in our culture and politics?

More importantly, should we care about elections?

Voting is very personal. It takes time to register and to learn about the candidates' views. On Election Day, you may need to leave work, stand in long lines, or slog through harsh weather, knowing all the while that the chances your vote will make a difference among the thousands—or millions—cast are pretty much zero.

So why do we bother?

Psychologists and political scientists have many theories. There are many factors why people vote. As a businessperson and a member of an association, a primary consideration should be:

- What do they know about my business?

- Are they focused on our business concerns?

For those of you with your own businesses, your days start out early and end late. You work every day doing something for your business, and often, a vacation is something you used to do before you went into business for yourself. The reason you hung out a shingle in the first place was to be free and have the chance to live the American Dream. So, you are wondering once again, why do we bother to vote?

With the passage of Obamacare and regulations on the state and federal levels, more and more who are in search of that American Dream feel like it's a nightmare. But these very issues are what makes politics closer to all of us than most people realize.

The people who get involved in issues and political campaigns know that who is or is not elected has a direct impact on their bottom line and realize it is worth their time and money to influence what decisions get made. They pay close attention to whom gets elected and sits in decision-making positions.

Many times, the people getting elected and making decisions that impact your business are people who have never owned or operated a business in their lives.

That is why getting involved in elections matters.

As the late Congressman Tip O'Neill said, "All politics is local." Nothing could be truer in elections on any level, and the corporation or association must make the connection.

If you connect issues, add your members and employees, then add legislators, and then add PAC involvement, you end up with relationships. These relationships built over time create centers of influence and allow you to be heard on The Hill.

Bottom line: Elections do matter. Candidates who get elected—and who make the decisions that have so much to do with every aspect of your life and your business—ought to be people who understand you and your business.

KEY TAKEAWAYS

- Follow your passion when voting and in life. Passion is what really matters in the end.

- It's important to elect business and issue-focused candidates based on what you or your organization believes.

- Be a voice for change. You may not change the world, but you can always learn something and change your perception of it.

- Listen to your voice in your organization, business, or personal life, and see where it leads. Sometimes there might be a chance to grow.

CHAPTER 9
Grassroots

"If you want the world ruled by law and not by force you must build up, from the very grassroots, a respect for the law."

First Lady Eleanor Roosevelt,
Writer and Humanitarian

CHANGE HAPPENS AT the local level. It is easy to feel intimidated by the structures of government or feel as though there isn't any way that you can make a difference, but the truth of the matter is that big change starts small.

Change begins when people unite.

They start out as one individual, maybe contacting their legislator, making a phone call, or writing a letter, but—when these actions add up—the results are significant.

When citizens lobby as individuals, or collectively, this is called grassroots lobbying. Anyone who participates in government by talking with an elected official on a local level is engaging in it. The key to success is being able to communicate your concerns to make a difference. Associations will often run campaigns to start a grass-roots lobbying movement in their favor. This is where an experienced lobbyist and a political action committee would come in handy.

A major ingredient of grassroots is educating the policy-makers about your concerns.

If you do not share your concerns with elected officials, then those views cannot be considered. No news is good news. If you say nothing, it will be assumed that there are no concerns.

This is the difference between having your voice heard or legislation moving forward despite your concerns. It will be because the elected official has never heard from you, either through a lobbyist, by phone call, or by letter. They will feel safe to vote in the manner that they feel is best. But what they see as best may not be optimal for you—and they may not even know it. They may have no idea of the disproportionately adverse effect the legislation will have on your organization.

Many times, I've had meetings with members of the Legislature and had someone in the room say, "If you oppose this legislation, then we need to hear from your association—today."

According to a 2011 survey by the Congressional Management Foundation, ninety-seven percent of congressional staff report that in-person visits from constituents influence their decisions, and eighty-eight percent report that emails also influence their policy-making decisions.

When I worked in the Pennsylvania State Senate, our office staff read all mail, and we regularly polled the district to get a pulse on what was happening and how people were feeling.

On an issue regarding the building of a veteran's home, the senator for whom I was working had concerns about funding.

Late one afternoon, a group of veterans came to the office from the Veterans of Foreign Wars (VFW), Disabled American Veterans (DAV), and the American Legion, to ask the senator to support building the veterans home. They came into the senator's office and spent over an hour answering questions. The time spent convinced the senator to support the project, and the legislation ultimately passed the Senate.

Grassroots efforts are the best weapon, and—if managed properly—can successfully reach and influence members of the Legislature.

In the past, political decisions were made primarily by a few in leadership, with little input from the constituency. Today, with social media like Twitter and Facebook, the focus is more on what is being said by local communities and the people who live and work there.

It is incumbent on organizations and their members to let their elected officials know their concerns. As voters, they have the most powerful tool available: their vote. An organization can hold each representative or senator accountable as a constituent. If your legislators do not hear from you, they will not know what is important to you.

Effective grassroots campaigns enable an organization to get their message across and help elected officials in making better—and more informed—decisions.

One of the most important aspects of our democratic system of government is that it is representative.

That is, those who make our laws represent us.

But how can they serve us if they don't know what we are thinking?

You can, and should, remind leaders of their responsibilities to their constituents and offer constructive feedback and ideas. Just being opposed to something for the sake of being opposed isn't helpful. If you have valuable insights and feedback, you can bring about change in public policy.

The issue of medical marijuana perfectly illustrates this idea of getting involved and grassroots lobbying. During the last few years, we have seen the rise of both recreational and medical marijuana legalization policies. Whether you are for or against medical marijuana, you cannot argue with the passion of the people who came to the Capitol to fight for it.

While working on behalf of an association, I saw this fight firsthand.

I was in the Capitol talking to legislators about legislation expanding the state sales tax, and during a meeting a state senator started talking about medical marijuana. I have probably been involved in politics too long, but I can remember in Pennsylvania—a state not known for being on the forefront of progressivity—when we couldn't even think about changing our liquor laws, let alone legalizing medical marijuana.

That same day, a group of at least 500 people came to the Capitol for a rally, and they did it again, and again, and again. That passion and unrelenting spirit translated directly into action. As I write this, Pennsylvania is just a few months away from allowing patients with major medical illnesses and conditions to legally obtain cannabis oil.

One legislative session focused on the opioid packaging limit. With an opioid and heroin epidemic raging across Pennsylvania, legislators were looking at root causes and ways they could limit the amount of these powerful painkillers on the streets. Hence, one bill sought to restrict the way in which opioid prescriptions were being written for workers' compensation cases.

At a hearing of the House Labor and Industry Committee—the group that deals with workers' compensation issues—business groups spoke about the cost savings for their workers' compensation insurance and the need for legislation. However, pharmacy managers and doctors spoke out against the legislation, indicating that patients in workers' compensation cases may unduly suffer without access to the drugs. Some of the largest political action committees and lobbying firms were involved in the effort to stop the bill from moving forward.

I was part of a small business coalition pushing for the bill's passage. We were not connected to leadership through our PAC, because most had small PACs in comparison to the other groups in the room.

We did not have any doctors on our side.

What we did have were our members, who wanted to see change enacted and had passion for their position.

If you take one thing from all these personal accounts, I hope you see that passion can move mountains—and sometimes more than money.

A vital tool for non-profits and corporations is grassroots or grasstops.

Grassroots make up the organization, but grasstops are the leaders in a community, organization, or a corporation. Both are needed at different times and for various reasons. One without the other will make it very difficult to move your issue from policy to legislation to statute.

When I think of grassroots organizations, the first that comes to mind is the American Heart Association. Most people have a friend or relative who has had issues with heart disease, and it is one of the leading causes of death in the United States.

It was because of a partnering of grassroots and grasstops that a nearly impossible piece of legislation was passed: the banning of smoking in public restaurants. It was a difficult fight, and it took a lot of time and effort, but passion is the kindling and fuel of any grassroots movement.

Then there are many other noteworthy examples. The American Civil Rights Movement was grassroots. When African-American leaders and activists marched on Selma and Washington, D.C., what they were really doing was lobbying. They were lobbying, or advocating, for their civil rights. They were advocating for their right to have access to the same treatment and the same public spaces as white Americans.

The Civil Rights Movement started small, with individuals and groups voicing their grievances. The movement continued to grow and become more organized until they were large enough and their message clear enough to be heard. Martin Luther King Jr.'s "I Have a Dream Speech" may be the most inspiring example of lobbying this country has ever seen. The Civil Rights Movement is one powerful example of the importance of grassroots movements and the way that passion and fervor can translate directly into political action and—eventually—legislation.

KEY TAKEAWAYS

- Grassroots is the process of individuals getting involved in the legislative process. Some grassroots campaigns can become very large when individuals band together.

- Lobbyists and associates might use advertising campaigns or community outreach to try and spur a grassroots movement.

- Grasstops are leaders who partner with grassroots movements.

- Medical marijuana legalization and the banning of smoking in public restaurants are both issues where grassroots campaigns had a significant influence on legislation.

- At the heart of it all, successful grassroots campaigns are passion.

CHAPTER 10
Legislative And Executive Branch

"It matters enormously to a successful democratic society like ours that we have three branches of government, each with some independence and some control over the other two. That's set out in the Constitution."

Sandra Day O'Connor,
Former US Supreme Court Justice.

A KEY COMPONENT OF the lobbying trade is the legislative branch and executive branch. The profession is about both whom and what you know. Most of the press is about currying favor and less about the need to understand a given issue.

A lack of understanding and communication can cause bad legislation and policy, even with the best of intentions. Access to the decision-makers is only half the battle. Having worked as a multi-state lobbyist, understanding how all of it works is much like understanding the fundamentals of hockey, soccer, lacrosse, or golf. Before you can go to the next level, you must have an understanding of the primary level.

My first encounter with the Legislature and its inner workings was when I served as the Executive Director of the Military and Veterans Affairs Committee in the State Senate of Pennsylvania. My executive branch experience came from working in the Policy Office for then Governor Tom Ridge of Pennsylvania.

The main committee system and operations of a bicameral Legislature are essentially the same in all states but Nebraska, so that part made my past experiences helpful.

One of my challenges involved dealing with a more moderate area of the country (Pennsylvania) and a more conservative area (Oklahoma). The state changes the nature of your relationships and how you deal with policy issues. Plus, Pennsylvania, along with New York and California, are full-time Legislatures, meaning they schedule sessions all twelve months of the year, as opposed to part-time Legislatures that may meet for a couple of months in a given year. That amount of time adds another layer to the mix.

George Will, a conservative commentator, has said, "When we have gridlock, the system is working."

Many of us believe that when we elect someone to office, we should expect to get things done on time and not string the process out over months. Whether we are talking about liquor privatization, pensions, or even the budget, gridlock seems to be everywhere.

Why? Isn't compromise part of politics?

Yes, but that depends on who is compromising with whom, and—like a marriage—there must be give and take on both sides.

By design, our bicameral system of government makes change difficult to achieve, giving control to the majority irrespective of the minority. At times, this may mean a more conservative, moderate, or liberal bent, depending on which party is in power at any given time.

One of the big factors in today's world is the influence of political campaigns. Regardless of what side you are on politically, legislators get elected by campaigning for office. They get elected by influencing and persuading the public they will represent them and understand their values.

This public opinion mindset is conducive to campaigning, but not to compromise.

Since the signing of our Constitution, public opinion has influenced policymaking. Even the Founding Fathers had to compromise to get a Constitution passed and prevent gridlock. Compromise is the bedrock of what we are as a country, even though that does not seem to be the case presently.

By nature, the budget, pension reforms, and liquor privatization are contentious and emotional topics because they touch the most sensitive of issues: work, family, personal responsibility, and community. These same issues often influence an election. Elect new lawmakers, along with new House and Senate leaders, and you have a recipe for gridlock. Many economists argue that gridlock on a federal or state level can put spending in check and help the economy. As frustrated as we all become by this, the impending "gridlock" represents a healthy and necessary indication that the system is working as it should and that the political winds are being slowed in their path.

I bet you can remember sitting in your high school civics class while your teacher talked about the steps and process of how a bill becomes a law.

You learned:

- Legislation begins as an idea. These ideas may come from a legislator or a citizen like you.

- When a representative has written a bill, the bill is introduced, and sponsors are added and assigned to a committee.

- When the bill reaches the committee, it is examined and reviewed by the members of the committee, or—in some cases—vetted by a public hearing. Once considered, the bill is reported out of committee, and if there is a fiscal note (meaning it costs the state money to implement), it is sent to the House Appropriations Committee.

- Once out of committee, the bill is put on the calendar in the House or Senate. Each bill must have three separate days of consideration. Amendments are routinely considered on the second day. On the third day, it can be voted on final passage. The state House records votes electronically, and the state Senate by voice votes.

- After both chambers pass the identical bill, it is sent to the governor where he can sign, veto, or do nothing, and the bill becomes law without his signature if the Legislature does not adjourn.

Not exciting, but you get the concept. Pretty straightforward, right?

Realistically, the process is not that straightforward and is why a lot of people become frustrated by both the method and the system. Aside from the annual budget—which can take up a great deal of legislative time—other issues are important. Subjects like pension reform, liquor privatization, ride-sharing services such as Uber and Lyft, and child abuse legislation are all on the table as major issues at the same time.

When the average cycle of legislation is between two and four years, and no more than five percent of those bills become law, it becomes apparent that—by design or default—waiting until the last minute to pass a bill is all part of our system.

If by now you think the Legislature operates in a crisis mode, you are correct.

Does it not make more sense to be proactive?

The legislative process has often been compared to making sausage or watching wallpaper dry. The biggest obstacle for lawmakers is like that of a hockey goalie who makes twenty stops in one game—but is judged by the one goal that gets past him.

Most all issues have both supportive and opposing sides, and the opposing party will employ delay tactics to bide time to make the bill more palatable (or hope that the topic is too hot to handle), and the legislation dies. And as more time drags on, the more intense the "crisis" may become.

The public gets upset with these delays and often suggests the

Legislature shouldn't celebrate legislative victories for simply doing their job.

Why should they when the crisis was self-imposed?

And still, others wonder: why did leadership wait until the last minute?

As is usually the case, whether in Harrisburg or Washington, D.C., your opinion of which party is to blame is probably determined by which party you belong to.

Meanwhile, Democrats and Republicans are growing more ideologically distant by the day, and that all adds up to gridlock.

It's not easy to pass a law, especially when passage requires a majority of votes in the House and the Senate and for the governor to agree. Getting everyone on board and everyone to concur—namely when it's an election year and everyone has a different idea of how to solve the problem—is going to take some time.

That wasn't in your high school civics lesson.

Now, you likely think there is no such a thing as "good government." It sounds more like a riddle—right up there with education funding and welfare spending, an endless cycle of spinning wheels. To unravel our mystery, let's look at some of the parts of government, starting at the state level.

In the legislative branch, which Legislatures are better? Those that are full-time or those that are part-time, meaning they have citizen-legislators?

With each state Legislature operating differently, it's difficult to paint this issue of "goodness" in black and white.

Being a legislator doesn't just mean attending legislative sessions and voting on proposed laws. State legislators also spend large amounts of time assisting constituents, studying state issues during the interim, and campaigning for election. These activities go on throughout the year. Any assessment of the time requirements of the job should include all elements of legislative life.

Many will argue that full-time legislators justify their existence by producing more legislation that covers more areas and appropriating more money than ever before. As a full-time legislator, there is a tendency for government to grow larger and more expansive in its quest to justify its existence.

First, these same people will further point out that a relationship between the growth of government and a full-time Legislature has caused a rise in taxes at the federal, state, and local levels—from ten percent in the early 1900s to almost forty-five percent today.

Plus, they will add that a full-time Legislature greatly diminishes the expertise that the citizen-legislators can bring to the legislative chambers. The full-time legislator, in contrast to those who work in the trades and professions and are part-time, has little idea of what impact programs being created will have on those they hope to benefit or regulate.

Second, arguments are made that term limits are the answer to good government. As a businessperson, would you shut down and fire everyone in your company every eight years because you want a fresh opinion? My guess is no. Why? Because you would have to retrain workers and would lose the institutional knowledge.

So, then, why does it make sense in government? You can still fire the people not doing their jobs: just vote them out of office.

Whether we look at a full-time or a part-time Legislature or argue in favor of term limits, one thing stands clear: voting makes the difference.

Some will argue that voting is not fair and is treated more as a privilege rather than a right, which is a discussion for another time. The real issue is that consistent change and the ability to be heard are still held in the power of voting. If you exercise your right to vote, you can make a difference—and that is good government.

KEY TAKEAWAYS

- The legislative process is like watching someone make sausage.

- Changing a law takes time, not timing. The bigger the issue, the more time is needed to educate the Legislature.

- The average cycle of legislation is between two and four years, with no more than five percent of those bills becoming law.

CHAPTER 11
Getting Started:
How To Choose A Lobbyist

"The secret of getting ahead is getting started."

Mark Twain,
Humorist and Author

AT THIS POINT, you may be starting to realize that you could really use a lobbyist.

And you're right!

There isn't any organization that wouldn't benefit from an in-house lobbyist. A lobbyist is someone fighting in your corner.

- But how do you go about finding one?

- And how do you ensure that you're partnering with the lobbyist that is right for your organization's needs?

In this chapter, we'll go over the process of achieving these things, step by step.

First, you want to make sure the lobbyist has experience. To be a good lobbyist, there is no magic number of how many years one has worked within the political system. However, many lobbyists have worked an average of six months in the Legislature—as an aide to a legislator.

On the other side of the spectrum, many legislators have left the Legislature to work as a lobbyist. These individuals have an insider's perspective into how the Legislature works, such as when a bill filing deadline date is and whether or not a bill can be introduced, due to states of emergency or a special session.

Second, the lobbyist should have a minimum number of contacts in the Legislature. Whether it is in Congress or at the state level, the lobbyist should be able to have a go-to legislator who can get a bill introduced quickly. However, the most successful lobbyist will not be limited to one party. Having contacts on both sides of the aisle will allow the lobbyist the opportunity to bring any bill, at any time, regardless of what political party has the majority.

Third, the best lobbyist should be strategic. He or she should be able to know when a good time to introduce legislation is. The lobbyist should know what legislator to target as the bill sponsor. This is important because the bill sponsor will be the champion for your particular bill, from start to finish. The lobbyist will need to educate the bill sponsor on the nuances of the bill, so that the sponsor will be educated enough to be able to respond to technical questions during a hearing or when the sponsor is in caucus meetings, explaining to their respective party about why your bill should be voted on.

The lobbyist should be able to pick and choose what committee will be best for your bill to go into and whom to use as strategic allies for your legislation—and be intuitive enough regarding when to negotiate and when not to.

Step 1: What is your budget?

This can be a sensitive issue, and no one wants to talk about money until it becomes a major subject. Money can often be a stressful or fragile topic. But it is necessary for business, and this is certainly true when seeking a lobbyist. Before you start talking to anyone, get an idea of how much you can spend and realize that the cost is determined by your market.

Like everything else, the cost for a lawyer in Los Angeles is more than the cost for one in Tulsa.

So, be mindful and reasonable about cost. You should go into your meeting with a range and keep this range in mind throughout the conversation. You should have both a ceiling and a floor that you are willing to pay.

Also, consider value. Don't just choose the lobbyist with the lowest rates. Sometimes paying a little bit more for someone with a lot more experience will bring you a better value. That is: you'll get more for the money you spend.

Value is a mixture of price and quality. If one lobbyist's rates are only slightly higher, but you feel that the quality of their work will be three or four times better, then choose them over the inexperienced lobbyist with lower rates.

STEP 2: REPUTATION

Reputation is something to consider when thinking about value. Lobbyists with stellar reputations bring better value with them. They have more to offer.

Be mindful of what others are saying about a lobbying firm. If negative things are being said, there is most likely a reason for that. By hiring them, you will take on their friends—and their enemies. That can be an issue, so make sure you are focused on their business integrity and their relationships in the Capitol.

If you pick the wrong firm, you may end up fighting the same issue for a long time.

STEP 3: DO YOU NEED A LARGE OR SMALL LOBBYING FIRM?

Size matters in the world of lobbying. Large corporations cost more but may offer less interaction. Small firms may have a capacity issue, and if you have a high-profile issue, this could be a big factor. The cost will correlate with size, so make sure to keep that in mind.

STEP 4: DOES A LOBBYIST NEED TO BE AN EXPERT IN YOUR FIELD?

Ideally, yes. If you are an energy corporation, you may want to hire someone who is an energy expert.

Lobbyists who are experts routinely contact people in the field and have access to the people in power. Getting your voice in front of an expert can be an extension of your company and can provide support on the main issues. Just remember that you take on both the friends and enemies of a lobbyist. Enemies are the people who can hurt you, so if a lobbyist has burned bridges—those burned bridges will become yours as well.

STEP 5: ARE THEY INVOLVED IN POLITICS AND PUBLIC POLICY?

As we discussed in earlier chapters, access is really about involvement. A lobbyist cannot provide access if they are not connected or involved within the system. A former majority leader in Pennsylvania, Representative Jim Manderino, used to say, "Everything is connected to everything else."

A lobbyist who is involved will be linked on many different levels, from within the Legislature or through organizations like the Chamber of Commerce.

You never know when you may need access to someone, whether an elected official or someone else within the scope of politics. When you hire a lobbyist, who is engaged in the process, you are providing your organization with options for access—options that you may direly need at some point in time.

Step 6: Do you need someone influential?

To be influential, you need to be in the game.

This means you need to have an active PAC. You need to have a high profile, and you need to have access to those who drive policy. These individuals are sometimes called "thought leaders." These are people like James Carville, Tom Ridge, or Haley Barbour.

With most everything in life, managing expectations is very important.

Regarding hiring a lobbyist, managing expectations is very important.

Be careful not to purchase what you don't need. If you have one issue, then pay for one issue, and not services you won't need such as tracking, branding, and PAC management.

Before you even interview a lobbyist, determine what you want and what you are looking for from the outset. Are you looking for someone to step in as a part of government affairs—or as a short-term contract lobbyist pushing an issue?

Once you've found a lobbyist whom you think you may want to work with, you want to ensure that your relationship starts out on the right foot. People are all different, and so expectations must be managed.

It's always best to be as accurate and honest as possible, and both parties should work to set clear and understandable guidelines.

So, let's go over exactly how to go about doing that.

Don't Assume.

Too often, both the lobbyist and the client believe that they understand the scope of the project. This can be an issue, because you cannot manage expectations that are not clearly spelled out. Take the time to ask questions and talk about your expectations. Pay for what you need, not what the lobbyist thinks you need. Set clear goals and talk about deadlines and services to be rendered. Yes, newsletters are valuable, and so are your website and bill tracking.

But the more options, the higher the cost, so focus on what you need specifically in the contract.

STEP 7: COMMUNICATE. COMMUNICATE. COMMUNICATE.

Communication is a big issue. It is important to correspond regularly, especially very early on in a project. This is even more important when working with a new client or team. Early on is when trust still needs to be developed; it is a relationship that needs to be nurtured and given priority. Checking in regularly gives you a chance to discuss the status of a project and manage any problems that arise. Often, communicating regularly will give you the opportunity to change expectations and deliverables.

It is always better to discuss changes than to miss a deadline.

STEP 8: KNOW HOW TO MEASURE YOUR SUCCESS

You need to ensure that you are comfortable with the expectations that have been set. Make sure that these are your goals and not the goals of your lobbyist. Set a specific goal. Have a way to measure your success. Maybe you will decide that you can count yourself successful when you have been able to secure the vote of at least five legislators on a piece of legislation. Maybe you will count yourself successful once your lobbyist has been able to remove two articles from an existing bill and introduce a new language into the bill that will not harm your business or organization.

Whatever your goals are, tie them to something specific, so then it will never be ambiguous whether or not you were successful.

One way to go about doing this is by using the S.M.A.R.T system of setting goals.

This stands for "Specific, Measurable, Attainable, Relevant, and Timely." Your goals should have a very specific focus. They should not be broad or vague but should be something that can be measured. They should be something you have a chance of achieving.

A goal is useless if you have no chance of reaching it. Goals should be something relevant to your purpose and the long-term mission of your organization. They should be given a time frame.

An example of a S.M.A.R.T goal might be: "I will speak with three legislators within the next month to discuss the pending legislation on employer-sponsored health care."

This goal is concrete and leaves no room for confusion. By quantifying the number of legislators to whom you will speak, you have an exact number to reach and to see whether you've been successful. By putting the stipulation of one month on the goal, you ensure that it is timely.

Step 9: The Interview

Make sure you familiarize the lobbyist with your organization and encourage them to visit your company or association chapters. Give the lobbyist background information and make sure to include the lobbyist in meetings with the government relations committee. Also, the lobbyist should regularly attend chapter meetings and board meetings to provide a report on his or her activities. Further, give your organization an opportunity to get to know the lobbyist by providing time for the members to ask the lobbyist questions.

Step 10: Contracts

Creating a contract is a good blueprint for the lobbyist, not only to establish direction but also to set a clear level of expectation. The organization should also design a performance assessment to measure if job responsibilities and expectations have been satisfactorily met. The lobbyist should be required to provide reports to the chapter on the progress of various bills.

You may also want to consider some of the following questions:

- Does the proposal cover monitoring of legislation only, or does it also include any given issue?

- Who will determine the primary issues?

- Will the lobbyist be providing both regulatory and legislative coverage?

- What is the term of the agreement?

- What provisions are in the agreement that cover possible conflicts of interest?

- What are the proper lines of communication to avoid confusion or conflicting information?

To best analyze the provisions in the agreement, you may want to have a separate legal counsel review the arrangement before signing.

KEY TAKEAWAYS

- Setting clear and tangible goals with your lobbyist will ensure your greatest chances of a successful working relationship. Talk about the entire scope of the project, from your big picture goals and deliverables to deadlines.

- Never make assumptions. Don't just assume that your lobbyist knows what you mean or knows what you are expecting. Everyone is different. Talk about everything.

- Determine your budget beforehand. Know what price range you are working within. Be sure to consider not just a lobbyist's pricing, but also the value that they will bring.

- Reputation is something that should be considered very seriously. A lobbyist's reputation will tell you if they have burned any bridges or made any enemies.

- You need to decide whether you will work with a large or small lobbying firm. A large firm may provide less one-on-one time with their clients. A small firm may not have the pull needed for a high-profile case.

CHAPTER 12
Strategic Plan

"The secret of success is constancy of purpose."

A Benjamin Disraeli,
Former Prime Minister of the United Kingdom

WHEN IN BUSINESS, lobbying or life, you need a plan. The plan is really your vision of what you want to do. An old Zig Ziglar story talks about a champion archer who would go out in exhibitions and hit the target dead center, and then when they blindfolded him, you would see the same result. The focus of this story is that you can hit a target you can't see, but you cannot hit a target you do not have. Former President George H.W. Bush used to call it "that vision thing."

A vision is your roadmap. This is not a mission statement; this is more than a mission statement. This is your core—it's your "why." Dexter Yeager, a very wealthy businessman with AMWAY Corporation, used to say, "If your why is strong enough, it can master any how."

The single biggest mistake in any lobbying strategy is to think you can accomplish your goal in three to six months. Yes—sometimes this is possible but remember that your primary reason for creating a government or public affairs program is for the long term.

Several years ago, while I was traveling extensively through my work at Sunoco, I was rushing to catch a flight when I received a call from the executive director of the March of Dimes, a client I once worked with as a contract lobbyist.

Dolores, who had become a close friend, wanted to talk with me about strategies to increase newborn blood screenings, one of the organization's signature issues. The March of Dimes had been working for years in each state to increase the number of tests done on newborns right after birth.

Significant research had shown that the earlier many genetic diseases and conditions were detected, the quicker more effective treatment could begin. In many cases, conditions and diseases could be treated effectively, leading children to have somewhat normal lives. Without the screenings, valuable time would pass, along with the children's chances of reaching adulthood. But convincing state Legislatures to expand the number of screenings—which would increase costs— would be an uphill climb.

Dolores and I talked about engaging key lawmakers—those who were familiar with the issue and those with significant influence—and she suggested contacting Jim Kelly for support with the program.

I swallowed hard and asked, "Is this *the* Jim Kelly: the Hall of Fame Quarterback from the Buffalo Bills?"

She said that it was.

Jim Kelly was raised not far from my hometown in Northwestern Pennsylvania. And since we're about the same age, I followed his career from a high school sports star in Clarion County, through his collegiate career and onto the pros. I was incredibly excited about the potential of working with him.

Even before his retirement, Jim Kelly has worked on the newborn screening issue through his Hunter's Hope Foundation. Hunter's Hope was established in 1997 by Jim and his wife, Jill, after their infant son,

Hunter, was diagnosed with Krabbe Leukodystrophy, a fatal nervous system disease.

Through the foundation, this Hall of Fame quarterback has done as much off the field as on it. I knew engaging him would be an excellent opportunity to make the issue of blood screenings less about politics—and more about helping people.

A few days later, Jim Kelly came to the State Capitol in Harrisburg and participated in a news conference—an event that attracted both print and broadcast media, not to mention hundreds of curious onlookers, legislators, and staff at all levels. Kelly talked about the importance of passing legislation that would increase the number of newborn screenings, and—therefore—help kids lead healthier lives. We continued to work the issue for the next few months, and eventually the legislation passed in Pennsylvania.

As a result of this legislation, newborns who have these genetic diseases and conditions are receiving health care treatments that may not have occurred, if both policy and public opinion hadn't been influenced by the collaborative efforts of lobbyists and public figures. Jim Kelly has a high profile, and that was a major influencing factor in public policy engagement.

This is just one example of how we used strategic planning.

At our core was our ability to collaborate with celebrities and public figures and how that helped to influence policy and public opinion—in a positive way. Unfortunately, I was in Oklahoma for business when Jim Kelly was in the Capitol, but his efforts made a big difference in moving the policy forward.

It will help you save money when hiring a lobbyist and will help your organization if you build government affairs or public affairs programs over time. When building an effective strategy, you should consider three fundamental questions:

- What do you want to do?

- Where do you want to go?

- How do you want to get there?

When I worked as a financial planner, I would ask these questions of anyone writing a financial plan. You must have a plan to have focus and a means to monitor your growth. If you did not have a plan, how would you know when you are successful?

What Do You Want to Do?

Keep in mind that when you look at a strategy, you need to look at all the demographics, including the impact of rural vs. urban and age vs. income. They all play a factor.

You are probably saying, "Why do we need to know this?"

These factors impact a given area and looking at everything will help you build and write a winning strategy for an issue or any problem.

The main point is that considering everything possible at the beginning, before you are engaged in an issue, will save you both time and money.

Where Do You Want to Go?

You cannot write a strategic plan unless you clearly know what it is you want to achieve. Do not expect the legislator to write and solve the issue for you. The legislator will help you, but you are the expert and the conductor of this train. Be sure you know where you want to go. Often, clients get an impression lobbying is easy: just talk to people and take them to dinner. Don't mistake easy for simple. The average issue takes years, and sometimes longer, depending upon what it is you want to accomplish.

How Do You Want to Get There?

If you have ever planned a trip for your family, the first question after you decide where you want to go is, "How do we get there?"

It sounds simple, but how you travel will determine when you arrive, and that is the same as a strategic plan. If your goal is to build an organization, then the plan should reflect a long-term strategy for building a government affairs program.

If the strategy is to fight a big tax or change a regulation, then that strategy calls for a short-term, all-hands-on-deck approach.

An association's strategy must be focused on what is important to its membership, and the strategy takes shape around that issue. People join organizations for information, training, networking, or the need for a change in legislation or regulation.

A few years ago, in Pennsylvania, the UCC RAC (Uniform Construction Code Advisory Council) recommended sprinklers be installed in all new residential homes in Pennsylvania. This single issue was a rallying cry for builders across the Commonwealth, with legislation being passed to revise this provision in the code, and a way for builder associations to increase membership.

Without members, associations cannot sustain themselves financially, but without members, they are limited in how they can win the issue at the end of the day.

Overanalysis Equals Paralysis

In golf, teaching professionals will tell you not to overthink a putt, because—if you do—you will start to doubt yourself.

More than ninety percent of putting is confidence.

An average issue can take two to four years to become law, and sometimes longer. The more you hesitate while deciding when to hire a lobbyist, it pushes that strategy out months or even years. Work on a long-term strategy, and if it comes together in less time, great.

Just remember, governance is not a sprint—it's a marathon.

Social Networking

The biggest phenomenon in the twenty-first century is social networking.

We live in a world where, through social media, you can

communicate with people all over the world, and it costs no money—just time.

More than anything, social media has changed how we interact with one another on a day-to-day basis. Not too long ago, a long-distance call was very expensive, and family reunions or funerals were the only time that people were able to get together. Now you can reach out to people at little or no cost.

For your needs, you must first establish social media. Some common platforms include:

- LinkedIn
- Facebook
- Twitter
- YouTube
- Google+
- Snapchat
- Instagram

The key to social media is to build a brand. For public affairs and government affairs, do not get so tied to the idea that it becomes a time crunch. Whether an association or corporation, your objective is to communicate with your audience. Some circles call this a tribe. Once you start to open communication, you can become an expert, and that is what you want to achieve.

The question is where you start in building a social network:

1. KNOW YOUR AUDIENCE.

Do not try to build all platforms. Start out and become an expert one at a time, but don't use more than three. My suggestion is Twitter, LinkedIn, and Facebook. If you are an association that advocates for health care, use social media to show you understand health care. If it's energy, use the media to demonstrate your expertise with all things energy.

2. Understand your objectives.

It is important early on to clearly understand what it is you are trying to achieve and how you will measure your progress toward those goals before you craft the content of your strategy.

Social networking is social, so you want to reach out to people who are in the best interest of your organizations. LinkedIn and Facebook will allow you to reach out to those people as specific targets. Twitter will allow you to reach the world, and Google+, Snapchat, and Instagram will let you build relationships with people on a more one-on-one basis.

3. Identify the best platform for your needs.

The selection of an appropriate technology platform will become far easier when you have gone through the first two steps.

Publicly open social networks like LinkedIn can be used to raise awareness about your organization and to attract potential members, but—more importantly—you can be seen as an expert. This requires thoughtful engagement and participation in established communities of interest relevant to your organization, even when they appear to be directly competing.

You need to be present wherever your members and prospects are meeting and communicating.

4. Measure results.

You cannot manage what you do not measure.

Fortunately, Internet-based platforms provide a wealth of information and metrics in real time, allowing you to obtain almost immediate feedback and to make adjustments early. When considering the success of a social network strategy, it is not just the number of page views or how many people have accessed the network, but how engaged they are.

Social networking does not replace marketing and does not replace the day-to-day interactions needed to grow associations or communicate with the public. Social networking is a tool, and—like any tool—it will work only if you know how to use it.

5. Metrics.

Social media metrics are data and statistics that give you insights into your social media marketing performance.

While some social media marketing metrics are universal, there are also platform-specific parameters you need to learn. Some data is calculated differently depending on the platform and social media metrics tools you're using.

Facebook offers the most comprehensive metrics for business pages. You can start by going to the Platform Insights page to see a list of your Facebook pages currently tracking metrics.

Twitter offers analytics for all account users that are easy to access, and LinkedIn analytics can be found by using an "analytics" tab to learn more about your post-performance and audience.

So, we have identified the three we should focus on.

Now, what should you look for when using social media?

While many social media experts recognize a multitude of key indicators, for your purposes, there are only two: audience growth rate and engagement rate.

Audience growth rate: is your audience growing?

Early on, you will want to grow out as much as possible and then filter out those that are not relevant to your business, association, or long-term goals.

Average engagement rate: This rate allows you to check and see if what you are posting is getting attention. Don't get hung up on shares, likes, and favorites, but instead look at the overall engagement rate. All social media metrics should be viewed through the lens of your overall goals; don't get so involved that you forget about your day-to-day business needs.

KEY TAKEAWAYS

- Understand what it is you are trying to achieve.

- Choose only three platforms to master.

- Do not try to build all platforms. Start out one at a time.

- Measure your results.

- Social networking is a tool and, like any tool, will only work if you know how to use it.

- Social media experts identify as many as ten key indicators, but for your purposes, there are only two: audience growth rate and engagement rate.

CHAPTER 13
What To Avoid

"Most people want to avoid pain, and discipline is usually painful."

John C. Maxwell,
Leadership Expert, Speaker, and Author

THE FIRST INCLINATION when an organization hires a lobbyist is to look at the lobbyist's resume and then employ the lobbyist who appears to be able to give you what you want— for the least amount of money.

But as with anything else, the adage, "You get what you pay for" does apply. As discussed in earlier chapters, you want to look at the value they bring.

Consider it this way:

You are thinking of purchasing a dining room set, and you have three options. One is from a bargain retailer, selling for $200. One is from a reputable furniture retailer for $800. Then one is from a high-end designer furniture store for $3,000.

You do some research and find that the $200 set is made of

particleboard and has abysmal reviews. People have complained of having the table break or crack apart after only a few uses.

At first glance, it appeared that the table was a great deal, at $600 less than the mid-range table. But after reading the reviews, you decide that you wouldn't be saving $600. Rather, you would be wasting $200, as the table will probably break and does not bring very much value.

In the same way, the $3,000 table is very small.

Its purpose appears to be more aesthetic than functional. This may be fine for someone looking to enhance the appearance of a room, but if your primary goal in buying the table is function, then—again—you will only be wasting money.

In this example, the $800 table appears to be best. It is sturdy and practical and will hold up for years. I'm not saying that the mid-priced option will always be best. What I'm saying is that you should not automatically choose the most inexpensive or expensive option. You should consider your needs and how price and quality will interact to create value.

You should do this with everything in your life that you pay for, but especially when hiring someone to advocate on your behalf. It's not a situation where you want to cheap out. "You get what you pay for" can have catastrophic consequences in this context.

As we discussed in the introduction, you also want to remember that lobbying is less about branding and more about relationships. Building a sturdy house requires it to be built on a strong foundation.

Relationships are that foundation.

Here, we'll go over how to properly build relationships with your lobbyist, with your elected officials, and in your community.

Understand the Issue

Never just jump into a discussion without having all your facts straight. Take the time and due diligence to collect research and be prepared to be challenged and cross-examined.

We've all seen the media news-storm that happens when a politician or someone of influence gets their facts wrong. People don't respond to emotional arguments, slippery-slope fallacies, or hyperbole.

The public looks down on those who can't be bothered to do their homework.

You want to build yourself up as a person of integrity and position yourself as someone who takes the time to understand the entire issue. There is a good chance that, at some point, your opposition will make a decent argument. They will have a good point and one that requires consideration. It will be better for you if you've already researched your opposition's talking points and you have already considered that point.

When you have all the facts and understand all the different ways of viewing an issue, you show the world that you are an expert and you are someone whose words can be trusted. Then, people will be more likely to listen to and consider all that you have to say.

DON'T LIE

This is just overall good advice for life.

People can sense dishonesty, even when they can't prove it. When you lie, or even if you just stretch the truth a little bit, you exude an aura of insincerity. People respond to those who are genuine. Even if the truth doesn't appear to help your case, when you come from a place of honesty and integrity, you will always have a better chance of getting others to consider your viewpoint.

Sometimes people lie because they don't think that they will be caught. Several conservative politicians and pundits found themselves in hot water when they lied about the contents of the Affordable Care Act, or as it is more commonly known, Obamacare. Sarah Palin was the first to falsely claim that the ACA would include the use of "death panels" to decide which American citizens should be subjected to euthanasia. [7]

This was—of course—false, and the politicians and pundits who

---

7 Holon, Angie Drabik. "Politics Lie of the Year: 'Death Panels.'" PolitiFact. Politifact.com. 18 Dec. 2009, http://www.politifact.com/truth-o-meter/article/2009/dec/18/politifact-lie-year-death-panels/

rallied behind this false claim lost credibility. Those in opposition to the ACA should have focused on the actual contents of the bill. If they had found something in the bill to criticize, they would have been perceived as having no actual argument to make.

These people were viewed as liars, or worse, people who make snap judgments without bothering to do any research. This makes them appear both foolish and immature.

While they had the attention of the public, they could have taken the opportunity to further their argument and explain to the public the real problems with the bill.

Instead, they undermined themselves entirely.

Don't Be Disrespectful

Politics is the business of relationships and people. Treat people well. If you anger or upset one person, you may end up alienating yourself, not just from them, but from everyone to whom they relate.

It is easy to understand why tempers may become heated and why people might lose their composure. As we talked about earlier, people act when they feel passionately about something. When you feel strongly about something, it is because it is connected to your core values. It is something that you really believe in and a part of who you are.

Even if you are arguing in favor of a bill that will help your business, you are still dealing with something that you feel passionately about. You feel passionately about your business. You want your business to thrive because it is your baby. You may want your business to do well because you want to provide for your family. Here, we can see the values of entrepreneurship and family. These are both incredible values to have, and it is easy to understand why they may move a person to action.

It is important to remember that this passion that you feel may be felt just as strongly by those who oppose you. Just because a person has different values than you do, or views the world through a different lens, it does not mean they are bad people. It does not mean they are worthy of derision or that you are justified in speaking down to them. It is also not okay to treat someone poorly or speak down to them if their debate tactics are not as strong as yours.

Perhaps they are relying too much on fallacious reasoning, such as non-sequiturs, straw-man tactics, hyperbole, or slippery-slope arguments. These are cheap tricks and have the potential to keep a conversation trapped in a loop of semantics and emotion.

But you must remember that your opponent is probably only employing these tactics because they feel so passionately. It doesn't feel great to be on the receiving end, but remain calm and assertive.

Don't lower yourself.

In this same vein, don't be passive-aggressive. Being passive-aggressive means implying something rude without coming right out and saying it. Passive-aggression is sneaky and underhanded because it does not allow the other person to respond to these implications.

If you are passive-aggressively implying that someone made a mistake, you are not giving them the opportunity to own up to their error. If you are just being mean-spirited, you aren't allowing them to call you out on your nasty behavior. An example of passive-aggression may be if you are speaking to a colleague who was involved in a filibuster only a few days ago. You may say something to them like, "Well, I hope we get out of here at a reasonable hour today. Some people just don't know when to quit. Then again, not everyone is married and has a family at home to take care of."

Here you are referencing your colleague's filibuster, and they know that. You are letting them know that you are upset, but giving them no opportunity to explain their perspective—or possibly own up to a mistake and apologize to you. Worst of all, you've made the attack personal, by bringing their marital status and home life into the situation.

These kinds of rhetorical tactics are mean-spirited and disrespectful. Acting in a passive-aggressive manner will make you seem both difficult and submissive. People often employ passive-aggression when they fear conflict or confrontation. People will see you as weak—as well as nasty. They will also be far less likely to consider what you are saying. They will be too focused on their feelings and thinking about the shoddy way they have been treated by you to consider your perspective.

In the political sphere, as in all areas in life, there will be conflict. But conflict doesn't have to be unpleasant and filled with attacks. State your positions and fight for them.

Let facts be your weapons, instead of barbs at the other party. Tear down your opponent's viewpoints, but don't tear down your opponent.

Treating other people decently is just good business. When you treat people poorly, others may see it and may not want to work with you. When you take the high road, people will have greater respect for you.

Even if others become disrespectful toward you, you can calmly state, "I'd prefer it if you keep your comments to the issue and not make it personal. I won't ever attack you personally, and I expect you to grant me the same courtesy."

People will not always respect your wishes, but then you can still feel proud of the way that you kept your cool. You can revel in the knowledge that you've acted with decency and integrity.

Don't Overstay Your Welcome

When you or your lobbyist meet with legislators, you should go in with a specific outcome in mind.

You want to be friendly and approachable, but you also don't want to be intrusive or overbearing. Make conversation for a bit and then jump into the issue at hand. Present your facts, state your case, and then clearly let them know the outcome that you desire. Maybe you want to obtain their vote on a specific issue, or perhaps you are aware that they have already positioned themselves in opposition to you. In that case, your only outcome may just be to get them to consider your views. You might say something like, "Will you at least think about the things I've said here today?"

If you receive an answer in the affirmative, then it's time to leave. If you overstay your welcome, you may intrude onto the time of those you are speaking with. If you irritate them or cause conflicts in their schedule, they will be less likely to be on your side. You also run the risk of them not inviting you back or allowing you to meet with them to discuss issues in the future.

CONNECTIONS WITH LAWMAKERS

One of the most important services that a lobbyist can offer to clients is their ability to connect with legislators and build relationships. A lobbyist should make it their business to network and get to know all lawmakers.

Nearly every business in America is based on the concept of networking. Networking is the ability to increase your size and influence through relationship-building. Networking is a trademark of sales at all levels.

Developing strong networks takes time, money, and effort. A good lobbyist can maximize your resources so that you can get to an answer quickly. Even if you would like to do all this networking and relationship-building yourself, with everything else that you must do to run your business, you probably just don't have enough time in the day to do it.

Networking is all about developing contacts, getting people to pass your name along to their associates, and belonging to organizations of like-minded people. These are all fundamentals of marketing a business.

The same is true for efficiently lobbying legislators. That foundation is built on trust, and it is as fragile as a piece of crystal. These points are like tools in a shed. Each one does something different, and—collectively—they help you to complete your task.

Often, people do not engage in government affairs until they have a problem, and then it is too late in the process to make a difference.

The biggest problem is complacency. People may think that they do not need to be involved in political affairs. They may believe that there is no need for a fix because nothing is broken. The problem is that can all fall apart in an instant.

When you have a lobbyist who has been laying the groundwork for your organization and fighting on your behalf all along, your chances of success are much greater when a problem does come along.

KEY TAKEAWAYS

- Understand the issues that you represent and position yourself as an expert in your field.

- Always be truthful: Never bend or distort facts. Do not cherry-pick facts or anecdotes to make your case. People don't respond to dishonesty. You will only hurt your own image and credibility.

- Be respectful of everyone with whom you interact. Never assume that you have the right to treat someone as less than yourself, just because they hold different views from you. Debates are full of conflict by nature, but that does not mean that you can't remain civil and keep your arguments based on facts and the issue at hand.

- Never stay longer than you are welcome. If you do, you may be intrusive or disrespectful of the other person's time.

- Forming connections with lawmakers is incredibly important. Networking is essential in nearly every industry, but it is especially vital in the world of politics and legislation.

CHAPTER 14
What I've Learned

"Success is getting what you want. Happiness is wanting what you get."

Dale Carnegie,
Writer and Lecturer on Self-Improvement

HAVE YOU EVER tried to watch PGA golf?

For someone not interested in golf, that can be a lot like watching paint dry.

Some of us watch golf to observe how others play and try to learn from their success, and—along the way—there are some life lessons.

Bobby Jones, the founder of the Masters Tournament and the greatest amateur golfer who has ever lived, said, "Golf is a game that is played on a five-inch course: the distance between your ears."

As kids growing up in northwestern Pennsylvania and raised by a single, widowed mother, my sister and I had to learn how to be resourceful. One summer, while I was experiencing the common feeling of boredom that most young kids feel from time to time, my mom showed me a set of my father's golf clubs. My dad died when I was only six, so getting a chance to look at his clubs meant a great deal to me.

The clubs were old even then, but they were my father's. So how they looked and their age didn't matter to me.

They were precious to me regardless.

The very first golf book that I ever read was *Golf My Way* by Patty Berg. I spent every summer in the backyard chipping plastic balls that would fly into the gutters of the house or over the garage into neighboring yards.

Although I will never make it on any PGA or Champions Tour, I did learn a lesson about effort and trying.

Even though you may never get the prize, what you learn along the way can change your life. Every time you take on a new challenge, you find out more about yourself and become a better, more well-rounded person. You enrich your life with every challenge that you take on, even if you aren't the best. The only person that you should measure yourself against is yourself. Those days in the backyard taught me about planning, hard work, and discipline.

Today, we live in a rapidly changing world. The rise of social media has altered the way to interact and communicate. We live on a twenty-four-hour news cycle, and whether we are talking about real news or fake news, the stories are coming at us faster than we can catch them. Often, an organization can be trapped in a media storm before they can even fathom how to respond.

But how an organization responds and how quickly they do so can have an immense effect on their brand's image. That response needs to be thoughtful and is the reason for this book.

Deciding to write this book was a real lesson itself. I never realized the level of planning, research, and effort required to get your thoughts down on paper. Aside from the obvious, there is another level necessary in getting this together—or running a business or a public affairs program—and that is execution.

It is amazing how many experts there are in the world.

Where is the implementation?

A great idea without a plan is just that: a perfect idea. Without action, ideas are useless.

Whatever your plan is, treat it like a business. Stay true to your purpose and build the plan around that purpose. The real magic potion is in good, old-fashioned hard work. I remember a line from the Broadway show, *FAME*, where the character said, "You keep on trying until you find something that works."

For anyone who has given effort, they will one day have a moment where it will make sense. Some circles call this an "aha! moment. " This is when everything comes together, as it finally dawns on you which strategy is best.

If something doesn't work, try something else. Life is all about trial and error. Learn new skills and then try employing them in different ways until you find something that works.

Progress and change happen when hard work meets opportunity.

You can apply this to an organization, a corporation, or as a life lesson. No one can deny this is a fact. If you have experienced this phenomenon, then you know exactly what I am talking about. It is an incredibly rewarding experience when you rise to meet a challenge.

I think perhaps another famous golfer, Arnold Palmer, summed it up best: "Success in golf depends less on the strength of body, and more on the strength of mind and character."

Lobbying has taught me that integrity and character count. It is important to know who you are and what you stand for. You need to have a clear and actionable sense of what your mission is.

Take every opportunity for growth that comes your way, and never shy away from something simply because it is hard. Hard work is good for you!

These are the lessons that I've learned throughout my career.

Next Steps

Building a government affairs or public affairs program requires a plan of action. If you fail to plan, you plan to fail. This could not be truer than when you create a program, or a business, on any level. Zig Ziglar used to call this being a "wandering generality."

First, think about what you want to achieve in the end and if that component requires outreach with the community. If your goal is to have a piece of legislation voted down, then you may go directly to the public to try and garner support. You may run ads explaining the negative components of the bill and how citizens, taxpayers, and business owners may be effected.

Keep in mind that without public affairs campaigns like these, many voters just wouldn't receive any information about these pieces of legislation. They may not even be aware of what bills are coming up in the House or Senate, or even in their state capital.

Most private citizens are much too busy raising their families or going to work each day to keep up with the many bills coming up for a vote.

This is why running a public affairs campaign can be beneficial.

It helps you to present your side of the issue, and it gives individual citizens information about bills that they didn't previously have.

Whether the entity is a corporation or an association, the most important component is in creating value. This could be creating value for shareholders or value for its members. That value is why you are in business.

Often, public affairs is best suited for corporations. When I worked for Sunoco, we were concerned about public perception, as well as the actions of legislators. Our refineries were in the community, and many times in neighborhoods. That requires community awareness. This is the same type of outreach needed for many Marcellus Shale natural gas drilling companies. They have this same challenge.

Government affairs is best suited for the association. If you are an association, your focus is on the value to members. Constantly delivering that value is what keeps memberships active and increases the number of new members.

In this case, what happens on a state level impacts your day-to-day business and your bottom line.

The example of an organization that does this the best is a state Chamber of Commerce. Its value is in fighting for businesses at all levels. From the environment to health care, to product liability, they are on the front lines.

Once you determine which of these forms of advocacy is best for your organization, then you need to start thinking about putting all the components together. All of the pieces are very important to your success or failure, so make sure you take the time to review and prepare.

Getting a director of government or public affairs will require both financial and organizational commitment. Just hiring one might fit the budget, but it may not fit your goals, and that needs to be considered as part of the process.

Aside from building the organization, your biggest challenge will be support from the organization. Lack of support comes when people don't see the value. This is where you need to ensure that you are properly communicating your value. Your message should be concise and easy to understand.

This brings us to our next step.

Communication is vital. No government affairs or public affairs program will survive without regular communication.

There needs to be ample and clear interaction with the board of directors of a corporation or the membership within an association. Communication comes from the top down. Those at the top set the tone of the organization.

Whatever your message is, you need to find a way to communicate that to all corners of the organization. The message should be consistent. There shouldn't be different leaders, or different board members, giving conflicting information. This will make your message muddled and convoluted, and your members or shareholders will not know what you stand for.

One way to ensure a consistent message is to have a mission statement. If you visit a corporation or association's website, you can often easily find it. This should include an organization's core values, as well as what they are trying to accomplish. By having a short, straightforward, and condensed version of everything that your organization stands for, you set the structures in place for a consistent message. No one should be able to stray too far from the organization's mission.

It is also important not just to write a mission statement and set of core values, but to emphasize their importance to the people belonging to your organization. You don't want to have a situation where your members assume that your mission statement is nothing more than lip service.

You can't just write a mission statement and then never bring it up again. It should be a cornerstone of all communications within your organization, and any additional organizational documents should be written with the mission statement in mind.

Then, hire the best and put together a program.

For many organizations, the primary focus is on the budget.

No one thinks you should overpay for what you want when hiring a lobbyist, but like buying a house, you need to think about the entire program. If you need to move a significant policy issue, then this needs to be taken into consideration. You may end up paying more but receiving a greater overall value.

"Plan Your Plan and Stick with Your Plan."

When I worked retail, years ago, my general manager used to say, "Plan your plan and stick with your plan."

When building your public affairs or government affairs program, these words make a lot of sense. Too many times, I see that once an organization gets everything in place, they become lazy and stop providing value.

Don't take the easy road and begin phoning it in. Don't make the mistake of thinking that just because you are starting to see some success, that means that the hard work is over. Remember what we said before: Hard work is good for you! Don't go around looking for ways to get out of it.

Continue to be diligent and hold yourself accountable. Continue to work as if you are still reaching for a goal. You should always be reaching for a goal. Once you have achieved your current goal, you should move directly on to the next. You cannot provide value to your shareholders or members if you are not constantly striving for improvement.

Don't rush or be hasty in your efforts. This process takes time and patience. It requires careful and thoughtful planning. If you are in too much of a hurry, you can wind up making errors in judgment.

The average program will take three to five years to put together, and at least another to see the fruits of your labor. As they say, "This is not a sprint. This is a marathon."

KEY TAKEAWAYS

- Decide whether you need a public affairs program, a government affairs program, or both.

- Create a detailed plan outlining exactly what you are trying to accomplish.

- Be clear and consistent in your communications. Consider writing an organizational mission statement or the creation of a set of core values.

- Understand that the most important goal you have before you is to create value. Know what your value is to your members or shareholders. This is always your number one priority.

- Be disciplined in your efforts, and do not ease up as soon as you start to see some results.

- Being passionate and genuinely caring about a cause makes all the difference.

IN CONCLUSION
Moving Forward

"Making an enduring company was both harder and more important than making a great product."

Steve Jobs,
Co-Founder of Apple Inc.

YOUR MISSION IN any organization is to build a program that can sustain itself when you are gone.

You want to put structures in place that are easy to maintain and consistent throughout the organization. You need structures that are successful and can efficiently move your agenda forward. If you redo, rethink, or restart your government affairs or public affairs program, it will never get off the ground. You will remain forever in the beta phase, and nothing can be accomplished from there.

Although these programs may not be the primary center of your organization now, they will be when a law is passed that you don't like or a regulation is forced through that hurts your bottom line.

We are lucky enough to live in a country with a participative system of government. From its very founding, the American system of government has welcomed involvement. The First Amendment of the Constitution guarantees the American citizen's right to participate in government.

> *"Congress shall make no law respecting an establishment of religion, or prohibiting the free exercise thereof, or abridging the freedom of speech, or of the press, or the right of the people to peaceably assemble, and to petition the Government for a redress of grievances."*

There is a lot covered here, but much of the First Amendment would apply to lobbying and the act of citizens involving themselves in the political process. Lobbying is legally protected by the "freedom of speech" aspect of the amendment. Grassroots political movements and citizen lobbying often take advantage of their constitutionally protected right to "peaceably assemble" or "petition the government for a redress of grievances." The suffragette movement of the early twentieth century employed both strategies, eventually affecting legislation and obtaining the vote for American women.

We are incredibly lucky to live in a country where we are free to jump in and become a part of the political process. Our government is not some high-and-mighty separate entity that is out of our reach. Rather, we can reach out and put our two cents in at any time.

Where a lobbyist can help is in navigating these structures of government. They explain how to use your two cents in the most efficient manner possible. They can guide you as to what processes to implement and who to connect with to create change and get a seat at the table.

I love being a lobbyist because I get to affect change every day.

I've had the opportunity to jump in and get involved in a variety of issues, lobbying for corporations and non-profit organizations alike.

My hope is this book has helped you to understand a bit more about what I do, and why lobbying is important. I hope that you walk away having a better idea of how lobbying is, at its very core, simply a form of advocacy.

The structures and processes of government need not be overwhelming and intimidating. You have a plethora of resources at your disposal. You could join an association, hire a lobbyist, start a PAC, or launch a government or public affairs program. These are all ways in which you could ensure that your voice contributes to the conversation.

Numerous people have added to the discussion around legislative action over the years. Many of these advocates have been able to band together and enact real change. Civil rights activists, suffragettes, those advocating for equal pay for women, advocates for mental health, and more have added to the discourse over the course of American history.

You can add to it too. You can have a say in what matters to you. No matter how big or small, you have a right to tell your government what is important to you, whether you are a business owner who wants to help legislators understand how taxes and fees may negatively affect your profits, or you work for an environmental advocacy group that wants to help lawmakers see all the ways in which alternative fuel sources could be implemented and the benefits they would have on the economy and the environment.

No matter who you are or what your interests and concerns are, you have a right to get them in front of your elected officials. All it takes is a little planning, organization, and some help from the right people.

Have you heard the phrase, "You can't fight city hall" or—in this case—"You can't fight a certain issue?"

Organizations often admit defeat and are willing to compromise before there is even a conversation about an issue.

Why?

The fear they will lose the debate and the issue.

Fighting city hall can be a very daunting task, but the only way you can even think about an argument is to develop relationships with the people in city hall.

Building a relationship with your elected officials is one of the most important government relations functions you can perform as a member of any association. When I worked for Sunoco, government relations was often the last stop executives would turn to when they had an issue. The only way I could help at the last minute was by relying on the relationships I had built with the decision-makers. Those relationships were built so that when the time came, I could get answers quickly.

Successful organizations with government affairs or public affairs make developing strong and meaningful relationships with elected officials a priority.

This success, however, must come from members of an association—members who are willing to take two or three minutes to write or call their elected officials and express their opinions on issues effecting them. That one note or phone call can pay huge dividends. Reaching out to your elected officials and talking to them about how issues directly impact your business really is a game-changer.

Elected officials are interested in learning more about your business and eager to meet you and everyone at your firm. It's their job to know their constituents and to understand the issues of importance to you and your business. As a business owner, you create jobs, pay taxes, and contribute to the community, and your elected officials have a vested interest in your success or failure.

When an executive director of an organization gives testimony on an issue, it often gets a little reaction, but it gets a business owner to make remarks—and all eyes and ears are on them. Because so much of your life is regulated at the state level, forming positive relationships with your state senator and state representative is crucial to the continued success and strength of your business.

All of this is a great tool in government affairs and grassroots, but it means nothing without the building of personal relationships with your elected officials.

It's all about relationships.